The Strategic Metals War

Also by James E. Sinclair (with Harry D. Schultz)
How You Can Profit from Gold

The Strategic MetalsWar

THE CURRENT CRISIS AND YOUR INVESTMENT OPPORTUNITIES

James E. Sinclair
and Robert Parker

ARLINGTON HOUSE / PUBLISHERS
NEW YORK

Inquiries should be addressed to Arlington House, Inc., One Park Avenue, New York, New York 10016

Printed in the United States of America

Published simultaneously in Canada by General Publishing Company Limited

Library of Congress Cataloging in Publication Data

Sinclair, James E.
  The strategic metals war.

  Bibliography: p.
  Includes index.
  1. Strategic materials.   2. Investments.
I. Parker, Robert, 1920-   II. Title.
HC79.S8S57   1983   333.8'5   82-11432
ISBN 0-517-54826-7

10 9 8 7 6 5 4 3 2 1

First Edition

Contents

1

The World of Strategic Metals

The commuter slipped behind the wheel of his Detroit-built sedan. Switching on an ignition system built with Zambian copper and Ghanaian aluminum, he drew on power from a battery of Missouri lead and South African antimony to start an engine of Pittsburgh steel strengthened by South African manganese and hardened with chrome from Zimbabwe. The car rolled on tire treads blended from natural rubber from Liberia and synthetic rubber from an Algerian petrochemical base. The exhaust from Nigerian gasoline was cleansed by Russian platinum. The commuter switched on a radio with its invisible traces of cobalt from Zaire and tantalum from Mozambique, heard a newscaster's report of a Communist-led coup in a small country in Southern Africa. What's that to me, he thought, switching to a station carrying the latest sports results.

THE ERA OF PLENTY

Like the fictional commuter, Americans for most of their history have enjoyed a worry-free abundance of most of the natural resources needed to sustain a standard of living that became the world's highest. In the early days of the Republic, the land readily yielded the food and fiber, wood and water to nourish, house and clothe a rapidly growing population. As railroads pushed across the continent, iron ore was abundant, along with the coal, coke and limestone needed to convert it to steel. As the age of electricity dawned, coal production expanded to meet the new demand for power generation. When automobiles developed their massive thirst for petroleum, enterprising wildcatters and developers met the challenge, and for many years discovered and produced all the fuel America needed and, until 1948, a surplus to sell abroad.

With good cause, Americans considered themselves a nation blessed with natural abundance, and in many ways they still can.

1

More than any other industrialized nation of the late nineteenth and early twentieth centuries, the U.S. could meet the most urgent of its mineral needs from within its own borders. Minerals that it did not produce it could easily import, and until the 1920s the nation enjoyed a surplus balance of trade in nonfuel minerals as well as in oil and coal. But two depleting world wars and the evolving technology of an expanding industrial network have made America a have-not nation in many of the most important industrial raw materials.

Unfortunately, for many of the U.S.'s mineral deficiencies there is no magic cure, no Spindletop oil find, no Mesabi iron bonanza to turn scarcity into abundance. For about two dozen minerals that are vital to both defense industries and to civilian economy, the U.S. must import more than 50 percent of its requirements. For dozens of other essential raw materials, dependency is less but still significant, and a total cutoff of foreign supplies would be disastrous.

DEFINITIONS

In dealing with the problems of mineral dependency, defense planners have developed a kind of shorthand vocabulary that it is important to understand. Strategic materials are those judged essential for defense and for which the U.S. is almost totally dependent upon foreign sources. Examples are chromium, cobalt, manganese and platinum. Critical materials are those also essential for defense, but for which the U.S. can meet part of its needs from reasonably secure sources within its borders or from friendly and accessible foreign nations. Examples are copper, nickel and vanadium.

In effect, the terms *critical* and *strategic* are used almost interchangeably, and most of the materials so described are essential not only for military purposes, but for thousands of civilian uses as well. So in referring to critical and strategic materials, we are not just dealing with problems of military procurement; we are talking about the essential raw materials needed to make computers and television sets, cars and locomotives, jet airplanes and oil refineries, pacemakers and typewriters and thousands of other machines that sustain our lives and well-being in the late twentieth century. We are also talking about jobs and prosperity, sanitation and health care, personal mobility, freedom of communication.

It is one of nature's ironies that many of the critical and strategic materials that sustain our society are found in abundance in only two areas of the globe: the Soviet Union and Southern Africa, one implacably hostile to the West, the other gripped by racial and tribal conflict, poverty, Communist subversion and conquest, and the turmoil created by the rewriting of economic ground rules that have governed world trade for a century.

The U.S. has choices to make. It cannot wait until the dust settles before arranging its future in a changing and tumultuous world. Plans must be drafted, legislation written and debated, investments financed.

There are dangers in the situation, and opportunities. We shall be dealing with both.

AMERICA IN TWO WORLD WARS

The U.S. went into World War I with no important stockpiles of strategic materials, but it received help from its allies, who were able to supply the U.S. with some of its needs in war materiel, and most crucially, warplanes and artillery. American manufacturers building for the armed forces relied on minerals produced at home or imported without great difficulty.

Although the American war effort was not seriously weakened by any shortage of critical or strategic materials, after the war some of the executives who had directed the industrial mobilization were convinced that the nation might be less fortunate on another occasion, and urged the creation of stockpiles of key materials. In 1921 the War Department drew up the so-called Harbord List of 28 minerals that had, in some degree, been in short supply during World War I. However, after the successful conclusion of the War to End War, the nation was in no mood to invest its resources in stockpiles of war materials it hoped never to need.

With World War II looming in Europe, the U.S. Bureau of Mines and the Geological Survey initiated a new study of the nation's potential problems in mineral supply, and in 1939 compiled a list of 39 critical and strategic materials—that is, materials in which the nation was in perilously short supply. That year, Congress voted funds to start an emergency stockpile much less comprehensive than the one envisioned by the agencies' experts. The Congress authorized and financed stockpile purchases of tin and rubber, supplies of which were threatened by the Japanese advance into Southeast Asia, and of industrial diamonds, chrome and manganese, then, as now, primarily products of Southern Africa.

The following year President Franklin D. Roosevelt, realizing the procurement program was far too small for the mobilization he planned, directed the Reconstruction Finance Corporation to create a subsidiary to be called the Metals Reserve Company, and to start buying war materials on a scale to match his pledge to create in America an Arsenal of Democracy.

One of the executives of this purchasing agency was Simon Strauss, later to become vice-chairman of Asarco, an international giant in mining, smelting and refining. He described the experience:

> By the time Pearl Harbor broke out, all of Europe was under the domination of Hitler. Africa, Latin America, Australia, India and even parts of China remained accessible to the U.S. The only competitive customer for the mineral exports of these vast areas was the United Kingdom. An agency called the Combined Raw Materials Board was created by the U.S. and the U.K. and a coordinated buying program was launched. It was possible to fight World War II without an actual shortage of these critical materials. But the key was the fact that we retained access to Latin America, to all of Africa, to most of Asia and to Australia. Had we been denied access to them, we would have been in trouble.[1]

Thus, in World War II the U.S. was blessed with willing suppliers, eager to sell their minerals to the U.S. and its major ally, the United Kingdom. In the early years of the war, chromite producers in Southern Africa stepped up their mine output to meet 28 percent of U.S. needs in that ore. But the problem of supply was vastly complicated by the presence of German U-boats in the Atlantic, which took a heavy toll in ships, cargo and lives in the early years of the war. However, by 1943 growing Allied naval strength in the Atlantic gradually reduced the U-boat threat, and war materials moved with increasing ease through the Atlantic sea-lanes.

Americans as well as the Allies mounted extraordinary efforts to meet the demand for scarce raw materials. In the U.S., some gold and silver mines were closed to free skilled miners to produce the more urgently needed lead, zinc and copper from domestic mines. Liquor distilleries were converted to make alcohol for the production of synthetic rubber. Large deposits of low-grade manganese and chromite within the U.S. were opened and worked, but without great success. The quality of the product was low, costs were enormous, and the mines were closed down soon after the emergency ended. Some of the low-grade ore from these mines later found its way into the national strategic stockpile, where it will need extensive treatment if it is ever to be used.

PROGRESS AND PRESIDENTS

Beginning with Theodore Roosevelt in 1909, most U.S. presidents of the twentieth century have addressed themselves to the problems of the nation's mineral dependency. Most ambitious of the presidentially sponsored studies was the Paley Commission report of 1952, which made numerous recommendations to government and industry for improving the nation's mineral reserve base. The report took strong exception to a policy of nondevelopment adopted in the name of conservation.

The Commission correctly observed that no developed nation can be truly self-sufficient in minerals. Perhaps its most notable service was to urge the federal government and the office of the president to accept responsibility for development of coordinated policies to assure the adequacy of the nation's mineral supply. The Commission noted: "The overall objective of a national materials policy for the United States should be to insure an adequate and dependable flow of materials at the lowest cost consistent with the national security and the welfare of friendly nations."[2]

Altogether, some 20 studies of mineral and materials policy have been made or commissioned by various agencies of the federal government. Their viewpoints and emphases have varied with the times and with the sponsoring agencies, but most have recognized, to some degree, the risk to national security in excessive dependence upon foreign producers for minerals vital to the defense and economic well-being of the U.S.

They have recognized the degree to which excessive foreign dependency deprives the U.S. of freedom of action in other areas: political, economic and defense. Yet most of these studies have realistically recognized that total self-sufficiency is an unattainable goal.

Confronted with this dilemma, most of the study groups have come out foursquare for better coordination of government policies affecting mineral availability, and some have urged greater government support for technological innovation. But almost without exception, American presidents have largely ignored these dutifully researched, carefully written reports to focus on issues of more immediate concern.

OIL AND DEPENDENCY

The nation's vulnerability to foreign mineral suppliers was never more dramatically clear than in 1973, when the Arab members of OPEC embargoed oil shipments to the U.S. because of Washington's support for Israel in the October war of that year. Non-Arab OPEC members, heartened by the consuming nations' feeble resistance to earlier price increases, joined the Arabs in quadrupling the price of oil in a single year, helping to trigger a worldwide business recession and a malignant inflation that still afflicts most of the world.

Still, neither the U.S. nor the other oil-consuming countries are totally helpless in the face of this producer-controlled price extortion. By removing price controls on oil, the U.S. government forcefully demonstrated to consumers the merits of conservation; at the same time, the prospect of profit for domestic producers touched off a renaissance in oil exploration that is leading to the discovery of resources at depths and locations never before explored. In the U.S., according to the Petroleum Industry Research Foundation, reliance on imported oil declined from a peak of 48 percent of consumption in 1978 to 36 percent in 1981, and consumption cuts elsewhere in the world forced a significant if possibly temporary rollback in world oil prices.

There are many parallels between the Western world's dependence on OPEC oil and its reliance on critical and strategic nonfuel minerals. There are ominous differences as well. With difficulty and at great expense, the U.S. and other industrialized countries can further reduce their dependence on OPEC oil. Through tax and investment policies they can encourage conservation and promote the development of marginal oil and gas deposits and alternate energy sources such as geothermal, solar and wind power.

But for many of the critical and strategic materials, there are no adequate substitutes at any price. Industrialized societies must have them or write off a good part of the technological advances of the past 75 years.

The most critical of these industrial metals, sometimes known as the Big Four, are chromium, cobalt, manganese and the platinum group of metals. One steel company executive, Robert Buckley, chairman and president of Allegheny Ludlum Industries Inc., put it succinctly: "Without these [Big Four] you couldn't build a jet engine or an automobile, run a train, build an oil refinery or a power plant. You couldn't process food, under present laws, or run a sanitary restaurant or a hospital operating room. You couldn't build a computer, clean up the air and water. . . ."[3]

These four materials have another point in common. Except for minimal amounts salvaged by recycling or in by-product recovery, none is produced in the U.S. In part because they are so essential, all are vulnerable to supply interruptions caused by boycotts, political disruption, sabotage and other causes unrelated to the normal commercial processes. They are at the top of almost everyone's list of source-threatened substances. The reasons are not hard to understand.

Manganese is an indispensable element in steelmaking. No one knows how to make steel without it. Added to molten steel in the form of ferromanganese, it removes oxygen and sulfur and hardens the final product. Manganese steel becomes harder with pounding, making it essential in steel for railroad equipment, rock crusher parts and the teeth of power shovels.

Chromium makes steel wear-resistant for roller and ball bearings, high-speed drills and dies. More chromium hardens the metal further for armor plating and weapons, while high-chromium steel becomes stainless, highly resistant to corrosion and retaining its strength and shape under the extreme temperatures encountered in oil refineries and nuclear and conventional power generating plants. In combination with nickel, chromium toughens steel for automobile connecting rods and drive shafts and for jet engine parts.

A study by the National Materials Advisory Board in 1978 stated:

> While [chromium] is an important ingredient in many commodities, it is irreplaceable in stainless steels and high temperature resisting superalloys, two classes of materials that are vital to the technological well-being of the nation. Currently there are no chromium-free substitutes that can be used in these critical applications, nor are any such substitutes likely to be developed in the foreseeable future.

Cobalt is, if anything, even more critical than manganese and chromium, in part because most of the Western world's supply comes from two weak and unstable African countries, Zaire and Zambia. Cobalt is an essential element for the manufacture of computers, television transmitters and receivers and most other electronic equipment. It is also an aerospace metal, used to fashion the vanes in the hot end of jet aircraft engines. Richard C. Mulready, an executive of the Pratt & Whitney Aircraft Group, has estimated that without cobalt from primary or reserve sources to manufacture spare parts, the nation's fleet of commercial jet aircraft would be grounded at the rate of 25 percent a year.[4]

Platinum finds its principal use as a catalyst in the control of emissions from automobile exhaust systems, but it has major applications also in electrical connections; in the chemical industry, where it is used in the manufacture of many products, including nitric acid for explosives and fertilizers; in petroleum refineries to improve the octane rating of gasoline; and in the manufacture of glass and fiberglass.

Beyond this short list of supercritical metals in which the U.S. is almost totally import-dependent lies a group of about 20 other materials, most of them metals, in which the U.S. imports more than 50 percent of its requirements and which are also essential for national defense and for the functioning of the nation's industries. This secondary group includes such workaday metals as tin, nickel and zinc. It includes some less familiar metals such as tantalum, antimony, cadmium and tungsten. But sorting out the relative importance of these metals and such important nonmetals as graphite and asbestos is a little like trying to figure out whether carbohydrates, fats or proteins are more important to the human diet. Industries need them all, just as the human body needs carbohydrates, fats and proteins.

The transition of the U.S. from the substantial self-sufficiency it once enjoyed to a have-not position in many key areas has been gradual. There has been no dramatic crisis in nonfuel minerals to compare with the oil embargo of 1973. With minor exceptions, the nation in peacetime has been able to meet its needs for critical and strategic materials through domestic production supplemented by imports, though at sharply rising prices over the years. How long the U.S. will be able successfully to shop the world's mineral supermarkets is a matter of considerable concern to the nation's defense planners.

The federal government's most decisive action to avert wartime shortages was the creation of a strategic stockpile, beginning in 1949. Ninety-three separate substances, 62 families of materials, were designated as strategic; each was to be purchased and stored in quantities sufficient to meet the nation's defense needs for a three-year emergency. But because successive administrations and Congresses failed to provide the necessary funds, the stockpile has never come close to meeting its stated goals. In 1981, total stockpile inventories stood at about 50 percent of the stockpile goals.

The purpose of the stockpile is to meet the needs of national security, not to serve as a budgetary balance wheel or even as a government profit center. But in fact it has made a bookkeeping profit over the years. Raw materials that cost the government $3.5 billion had risen in value by 1981 to $12.56 billion.[5]

Political realism suggests that the budget-conscious Reagan Administration is unlikely to recommend purchases on such a scale in the absence of a clear and obvious national emergency. The alternative adopted in 1981 was to sell off surplus tin and silver to raise funds to buy cobalt and titanium. Whether some future technological twist will lead the stockpilers once again to repurchase materials they have sold is an open question.

One who has voiced alarm at the state of the strategic stockpile is General Alton D. Slay, who until his retirement in 1981 was commander of the Air Force Systems Command, in effect the chief procurement officer for the Air Force. In November 1980 he told the Industrial Preparedness Panel of the House Armed Services Committee:

> The critical materials stockpile represents much more than an assurance of adequate supplies in times of national emergency. It also represents great savings in lead times, manpower, energy, production capacity, scarce machinery, and transportation incident to mining and processing these materials in time of national emergency. An adequate stockpile would eliminate demands that would otherwise create additional constraints in a wartime environment.[6]

In his presentation to the panel, General Slay called attention to a "dangerous flaw" in the nation's defense preparedness posture: the heavy dependence on the unstable region of Southern Africa for cobalt, chromium and manganese. He said:

The adoption of Marxist regimes by five African countries south of the Sahara has contributed to the political instability of this region and the likelihood of future supply disruptions. Only a few more nations would have to fall under Soviet influence for the elements of a supercartel to coalesce. Control of these primary sources of strategic mineral reserves means the power to gain political and economic concessions through the manipulation of supplies to consumer countries.[7]

General Slay is only one of many experts who feels that the Soviet Union is waging a "resource war" with the double-edged purpose of securing unlimited access to the world's scarce natural resources for the Soviet Union and its friends and denying those resources to the West. Congressman David Marriott, ranking Republican on the House Mines and Mining subcommittee, quotes an unnamed observer: "From the Soviet point of view, a resource war is low-cost, low-risk, low-casualty, low-visibility and almost below the threshold of Western response."

Others have cited the statements of Soviet figures from Stalin to Brezhnev to a recent defector from the KGB to demonstrate that reaching out for raw materials and denying them to the West has become a major motivating force in Soviet policy, applying with especial force in the mineral-rich regions of the Middle East for oil and Southern Africa for nonfuel minerals.

It is an assumption of the authors of this book that such a resource war is a reality. The evidence will be examined more closely in another chapter.

SOME PROBLEMS AND SOLUTIONS

So far this discussion has focused on the formidable problems that face U.S. policymakers and indirectly confront U.S. citizens, voters and consumers. Some conclusions begin to emerge.

Failure to solve the supply problem for critical and strategic materials will weaken the U.S. militarily and economically. At worst, security of the country will be threatened. At best, jobs will be lost, inflationary pressures will increase, and the standard of living will suffer because of reduced industrial efficiency, lowered health care standards and declining quality in the transportation and communications systems.

It is pointless to look back nostalgically to a nineteenth-century concept of self-sufficiency. The clock runs in only one direction, and not only have many once rich resources become depleted, but changing technology demands new and different resources.

The difficulties that the nation faces should not, however, obscure one important point. The U.S. is still enormously productive in raw materials. It is not only the world's leading producer of food, but it also leads in production of natural gas, copper and molybdenum and is second largest producer of coal, lead and uranium, the third-ranking producer of oil and zinc. In total, it produces about one-fourth of the world's output of raw and processed minerals. But its needs beyond these basic materials are so enormous that it must continue to seek and develop sources for the vast array of raw materials in which it is partly or totally import-dependent.

The nation's needs for raw materials will continue to grow in volume with the population and in complexity with the growth in technology. At the same time, intelligent choices can reduce its dependency on certain raw materials.

If the U.S. is further to reduce its dependence on imported oil, it may need to develop an efficient battery-powered automobile. This is a dream long held by basement inventors as well as by major automobile manufacturers, but the major obstacle has been the great weight of conventional lead-based storage batteries. One channel of investigation lies in the development of a lightweight fuel cell with a technology based on lithium, the lightest of the metals. The U.S. is relatively well stocked with lithium reserves, but if demands for the metal should multiply, the nation may need to turn to Chile and Zaire, also holders of substantial reserves of lithium.

Evolving technology is constantly changing industry's requirements for specific metals. The cast iron used to make exhaust valves for early automobiles broke down under the higher temperatures of aircraft engines as early as World War I. This led to development of cobalt alloys to meet the new stresses. As interior temperatures of engines rose with performance demands, other alloys using varying proportions of chromium, nickel and cobalt were developed, some also requiring molybdenum, tungsten, columbium and tantalum. The name *superalloy* was given to this group of metals, which are esential for the fabrication of the hot working parts of rocket engines, jet turbines and nuclear reactors.

The development of the jet engine alone has added substantially to the demand for nickel, chromium, cobalt, tantalum, columbium and titanium. This latter metal, titanium, in fact, represents nearly 30 percent of the weight of the Pratt & Whitney JT8D engine[8] which powers most of the commercial jets flying in the U.S. and American-built aircraft abroad. Titanium is one-third lighter than steel, offering advantages in fuel efficiency and performance. Each generation of aircraft uses a higher proportion of titanium in its over-all weight, and this trend seems likely to continue, generating huge future demands for this metal.

The Soviet Union was a substantial supplier of titanium metal to the U.S., but without explanation it began to cut back sales in the 1970s, reportedly because the Soviets were using large amounts of titanium to fabricate the hulls of submarines of a new and advanced design and for their aerospace program. How willing would the So-viets be to provide additional tonnages of titanium to help the U.S. built a new high-speed bomber like the B-1? Assuming that the an-swer is obvious, U.S. producers are stepping up production of ti-tanium sponge, the basic raw material from which titanium metal is made. With titanium, the U.S. is fortunate; it has reserves of ore and is getting manufacturing facilities geared up, though it will also likely have to increase purchases of ore from Australia and sponge from Japan.

Newer technologies will generate demand for still other rare and obscure elements, some of them less known as industrial materials than as laboratory curiosities. Gallium is one of these. The U.S. in 1981 consumed around eight metric tons of gallium, mainly to make light-emitting diodes for the dials of calculators, clocks, television sets and instruments. The U.S. imported about 40 percent of its requirements in gallium, at a 1981 price that hovered around $630 a kilogram. Gallium arsenide cells show a promising potential for achieving efficient generation of electric power from the sun, and the House Mines and Mining subcommittee has published an esti-mate that 25,000 metric tons of gallium will be required between 1991 and the year 2000 for solar power generation.

Germanium is another element with an obscure past and a fas-cinating future. Recovered as a trace element in base metal mining, it was produced in the U.S. at an annual rate of seven to ten metric tons during the mid-1970s. The development of new applications in light-emitting diodes and in fiber optic technology—the transmis-sion of data by means of light traveling through transparent fibers—boosted demand and consumption.

At the same time, the Soviet Union, a former supplier, cut back its sales, prompting speculation that it was using its production of germanium to arm its expanding tank fleet with night sights. The price of germanium rose from around $293 a kilogram in the mid-1970s to around $800 in mid-1982. The price of germanium rests more on the cost of production than on any real scarcity, and given a market and a price, adequate supplies will be available from base metal ores and from the treatment of ash and flue dusts left from the burning of some coals.

WASHINGTON VOICES

One of the Washington groups most actively concerned with developing solutions to the problems of material shortages is the House subcommittee on Mines and Mining, headed by Nevada's James Santini. The subcommittee is part of the Committee on Interior and Insular Affairs, but Santini has made his subcommittee a semi-independent voice on questions involving nonfuel minerals. In 1980, after a tour of Southern Africa by subcommittee members and staff, the group made a series of recommendations for dealing with what the subcommittee called "the self-defeating nonfuel minerals nonpolicy that is crippling the United States mineral industry, increasing national dependence on foreign sources, and placing in jeopardy the nation's economy, defense and world stature."

The subcommittee recommended creation of an Office of Energy and Minerals within the Executive Office of the President or in the Office of Management and Budget, to make sure that questions of mineral supply are given due weight in top-level policy making. The subcommittee further recommended that the Department of the Interior should make public lands more accessible for mineral exploration and development; that the tax laws be changed to encourage investment in domestic mineral industries; that environmental standards applied to mineral industries be "economically attainable"; and that foreign policy should take into greater account the mineral requirements of the U.S.

To these recommendations, at least one other might well be added: the adoption of laws and regulations to encourage the private as well as the public stockpiling of critical and strategic materials.

STRATEGIC METALS AS INVESTMENTS

For many centuries, individuals have bought and held gold and silver as personal investments, as a hedge against inflation, as an economic safeguard against adversity. Many of the strategic materials are also extremely valuable on a per-ounce or per-kilo scale. If gold, a cherished but essentially useless metal, can constitute a durable, inflation-resistant storehouse of value, so also can platinum, an almost equally costly and far more useful substance with countless industrial applications and importance to national defense as a strategic metal. So also can several others of the platinum group of metals; also gallium, germanium, tantalum, columbium and many others of the most rare and critical industrial metals. The private stockpiling of these metals can contribute to the security of the U.S. if a materials emergency arises. It can also contribute to the financial security of investors. The investment potential of critical and strategic materials is an idea whose time has come.

2

The Special Importance of South Africa

Foreign policy should include the legitimate economic interests of the United States as a significant element of its
national security interests.
—House Subcommittee on Mines and Mining,
    November 1980[1]

Even before his election as president, Ronald Reagan made it clear
that he would assign a high priority to the pursuit of U.S. economic
interests abroad, and in particular to the assurance of a safe and
secure supply of critical and strategic materials. Early in the presidential campaign of 1980, he appointed a Strategic Minerals Task
Force to evaluate past policies on strategic minerals and recommend
new approaches to the problem of mineral supply. While the report
of the Task Force remained a confidential document, it became clear
very early in the new Administration that President Reagan assigned
a high priority to the solution of problems that the Task Force had
addressed. His concern was reflected in a number of key appointments: James Watt as secretary of the interior; Murray Weidenbaum, an economist who had written and spoken on the subject, as
chief of his Council of Economic Advisors; and a number of sub-
cabinet appointments in the departments of Interior and State.

In no area of policy is the issue of critical and strategic materials
more crucial than in U.S. relations with the nations of Africa, and in
particular those in the continent's southern third. The great plateau
of Southern Africa, extending from South Africa's Transvaal province
to Zaire's Shaba province, shelters the world's richest treasure in
critical and strategic materials, rivaled only by the riches of Soviet
Siberia. Southern Africa is frequently called the Persian Gulf of minerals, and South Africa its Saudi Arabia.

The region is also a crazy quilt of national boundaries inherited
from colonial regimes; of tribal rivalries older than recorded history;
of cruel poverty and vast resources; of hunger among abandoned

15

farms; of roads and railroads that the jungle has reclaimed; of once rich mines slipping into dangerous disrepair. It is a cockpit of racial animosities with political opportunists of all colors seeking to capitalize upon them. The region's governments include some reasonably democratic regimes as well as a number of Marxist states, a military dictatorship or two and some regimes less concerned with ideology than with staving off starvation in the countryside until the next harvest. Many of the black nations are united by little except their desperate need for capital and development, transportation and food, a shared suspicion of the West, and a common hostility to the most powerful state in their region, white-ruled South Africa.

This for the West is also a region of vital importance, the funnel end of a lifeline that provides most of the chromium, manganese, platinum and cobalt consumed by the industrial West. It has importance for the deposits of other critical minerals that are scattered through the region, some developed, some discovered but undeveloped, others only a gleam in the eye of geologists.

South Africa is a land rich with gold and platinum; with enough diamonds to adorn the women and edge the cutting tools of the world for centuries to come; with lead, zinc, tin, silver and uranium; with cadmium, copper, columbium, tantalum, coal and iron. It produces more than 50 minerals from some 900 mines and quarries. Without doubt it could further expand its known resources by the simple expedient of searching them out with the sophisticated tools of modern geology, or in some cases by reworking old mine dumps. From old gold mine dumps South African companies are producing not only commercial quantities of previously unrecovered gold, but significant amounts of uranium and enough cobalt to make the country self-sufficient in this important metal by the mid-1980s. South Africa's problem clearly is not a lack of resources; its concern is to guard its security against internal and external threats and thus to assure an environment in which it can continue to prosper and to supply its customers in Western Europe, the U.S. and Japan.

While to much of the world South Africa is synonymous with mineral wealth and racial tension, it is a land remarkable for its accomplishments as well as its endowments. Settled by Dutch and English pioneers who fought each other in a war for dominance, it became an island of white rule, brooding at the tip of a continent of brown and black. Its 28 million residents, only 16.2 percent of them white, collectively enjoy the highest living standards and the longest lives on the African continent. Only 7 percent of Africa's population, they produce 20 percent of its goods and services, 40 percent of its industrial output, 86 percent of its steel, more than half of its electrical power; they account for 42 percent of its telephones, 43 percent of its registered motor vehicles,[2] and close to a quorum of its political controversies.

While South Africa is richly endowed in minerals, in fertile farmlands, in climate and in able industrial leaders, its history has conferred upon it one of the world's most intractable social conflicts. South Africa's system of apartheid (apartness), developed and institutionalized largely by the Afrikaans-speaking majority within the white minority, lodges in the hands of the nation's 4.5 million whites virtually all political power and economic control. South Africa's 23.5 million blacks, Coloureds (persons of mixed race) and Asians may not vote in national elections; they may reside only in areas designated for them by the national government, and though joblimitation laws are gradually being relaxed under pressure of a national labor shortage, nonwhites are barred from holding many of the nation's executive and white-collar jobs, and even many of the better-paying blue-collar jobs. Africans must carry identification papers, complete with fingerprints, and be prepared to show these passes to a policeman on demand. Government per capita expenditures for black education, health and housing are only a fraction of the per capita outlays for these services for whites. The lives of nonwhites are thus greatly circumscribed by a government they cannot control through the ballot.

Countless books and documentary studies have examined the history and social effects of apartheid, and this book will not repeat that material except as it bears on its principal theme. But the issue of apartheid is so pervasive in South Africa and such a major irritant in the nation's international relations that it cannot be ignored.

While social change and the pressures of an expanding economy have opened to blacks many jobs formerly held only by whites, all change stops short of conferring true political power on nonwhites. Political equality would, in the view of the whites, constitute the first step to converting South Africa to black rule. This is unacceptable to most white South Africans, and emphatically so to the ruling National party.

Because of the rigidities in the system, blacks seeking political power must operate largely outside the framework of law, and many young militants have gravitated to such organizations as the African National Congress and the Pan-Africanist Congress. Both organizations have been suppressed since 1960 and so largely operate from bases outside South Africa to promote change—revolution, in the view of most white South Africans—inside the nation. To an extent they fill the role that in other countries is played by an elected opposition.

Without a doubt some of the illegal organizations are financed and encouraged by Moscow, raising the question of what kind of political system they would install if they succeeded in overthrowing the government. However, such an overthrow seems quite remote from the perspective of 1982. With an efficient police force and well-trained and well-equipped armed forces that do not hesitate to cross borders to raid guerrilla camps, the South African government feels confident of its ability to control internal insurrection. "We can deal with anything but an Afghanistan," says a South African official. What may be more difficult to combat is politically inspired sabotage, such as the simultaneous bomb attacks on two of South Africa's synthetic fuel plants that occurred in 1980.

THE U.S. AND SOUTH AFRICA

For the last three decades, roughly the period that the National party has ruled South Africa, U.S. policy toward South Africa has swung on a pendulum, basically from a laissez-faire policy of noninterference under conservative presidents to an active, ideologically based policy under presidents Kennedy and Carter. In 1952, when the first antiapartheid resolution was put before the United Nations, Eleanor Roosevelt, then a member of the U.S. delegation, urged support for the resolution, but in the end she was overruled by Secretary of State Dean Acheson, who felt that the U.S. "should not intervene for what are called moral reasons in the internal affairs of another country." The U.S. delegation abstained on the resolution, while Britain and France opposed it.

South Africa, an important source of uranium, became a member of the International Atomic Energy Board, and thus gained access to much classified technical information developed by American scientists. An American firm, Allis Chalmers, constructed South Africa's first research reactor, which went into service in 1965.

On March 21, 1960, in the African township of Sharpeville, 35 miles south of Johannesburg, a demonstration against the pass system was broken up by police, who fired into the crowd of demonstrators, killing 67 Africans, including some women and children. In Washington, the State Department issued a statement regretting the "tragic loss of life" and expressing the hope that "the African people of South Africa will be able to obtain redress for their legitimate grievances." The U.S. called a meeting of the U.N. Security Council and joined a unanimous vote (Britain and France abstaining) expressing the view that the South African situation "might endanger international peace and security."

During the Kennedy Administration, the U.S. government informed Pretoria that it would be unable "to cooperate with South Africa in ways which would lend support to apartheid," but on military and strategic matters the U.S. extended quiet cooperation. American naval ships called in South African ports, and an agreement was reached leading to the establishment of a space-tracking station in South Africa. The U.S. also agreed to sell arms to South Africa "for use against Communist aggression."

In 1967, the aircraft carrier *Franklin Delano Roosevelt*, homeward bound from combat duty off Vietnam, was scheduled to call in Capetown for fuel and for shore leave for the ship's battle-weary crew. As it happened, the scheduled visit coincided with a meeting in Washington of the American Negro Leadership Conference on Africa. The issue quickly involved members of Congress and senior members of the Administration of President Lyndon Johnson. The captain of the *Roosevelt* was directed to ensure that shore-leave activities of the crew be on an integrated basis only. The captain found that this was impractical, and so put into port only long enough to take on fuel, without extending shore leave to the crew. Since that time, U.S. naval vessels have called in South Africa only in emergencies.

During the Nixon Administration, Henry Kissinger, then the White House security advisor, ordered a review of U.S. policy toward South Africa and eventually endorsed what came to be known as Option Two, which in reference to South Africa stated:

> The whites are here to stay and the only way that constructive change can come about is through them. There is no hope for the blacks to gain the political rights they seek through violence. We can, through selective relaxation of our stance toward the white

regime, encourage some modification of their current racial and
colonial policies. . . . Our tangible interests form a basis for our
contacts in the region, and these can be maintained at an acceptable political cost. [3]

Without announcing any policy shift, the Nixon Administration
quietly sold light planes, troop transports, communication equipment and other military hardware to South Africa, and welcomed
the chief of the South African Defense Force, Admiral Hugo Bier-
mann, to the Pentagon. The Department of Commerce shifted from
"neither encouraging nor discouraging" American investment in
South Africa to a stance encouraging American businesses in South
Africa to adopt progressive policies toward their employees. But the
move that did most for South Africa was one entered into for totally
different reasons. It was the U.S. decision to abandon its attempt to
control the price of gold and to allow the world price to float up in
response to market forces. Gold moved up to a range of $200 an
ounce by 1974, and up to a peak of $887.50 an ounce in early 1980.
As the producer of about 55 percent of the world's newly mined
gold, South Africa enjoyed enormous financial benefits from these
unprecedented prices for its leading export commodity.

The question of arms sales continued to trouble U.S. policymakers. But in 1977, when the U.N. declared a mandatory embargo
on arms sales to South Africa, the newly installed Carter Administration willingly complied. The U.S. applied a broad definition of arms,
and declared an effective embargo against the sale not only of weapons but of any equipment designed to aid the South African defense
forces and police forces charged with enforcing the nation's apartheid laws. In addition, the Import-Export Bank denied loans to support sales of any kind to South Africa.

There was no question that South Africa was able to buy most of
the arms and equipment it needed through private intermediaries or
back-door transactions. At the same time, the South African government increased its domestic production of many of the items it
needed, including a long-range armed personnel carrier operating
on wheels at high speed in rough terrain. Producing about 300 of
these vehicles a year, South Africa was expected not only to provide
for its own needs but to develop a surplus for export sales.

While the principal thrust of the Carter Administration's policies
toward South Africa was to press for internal reform, the Admin-

istration showed little concern for a problem that was beginning to trouble many individuals in the private sector and in the defense-related establishment. This was the question of closing the widening gap between America's needs for critical and strategic materials and the safe and assured sources upon which the nation had long relied.

The period of the Carter Administration was a particularly tense time for U.S.–South African relations, as Carter, his secretary of state, Cyrus Vance, and two successive ambassadors to the United Nations, Andrew Young and Donald McHenry, all were committed to "doing something about South Africa." At the State Department, the African Bureau, headed by Assistant Secretary Richard Moose, saw black African nationalism as a major historical force operating on the continent, whose ultimate triumph even in South Africa was inevitable.

The prevailing view was that the U.S. should work with this force, not against it, as a means of slowing and thwarting Soviet imperialism in Africa, and in the long run making it possible for whites to continue to live in Southern Africa. Andrew Young in particular rarely bothered to veil his deeply felt convictions with diplomatic discretion, and once in a casual reply to a journalist's question agreed to a characterization of the South African government as "illegitimate." Although the State Department disavowed the statement, a South African National party newspaper decided, "There is no doubt that relations between South Africa and the United States of America have reached an all-time low."[4]

Matters were scarcely improved when Vice-President Walter Mondale, at a meeting in Vienna, warned Prime Minister John Vorster that South Africa must take steps toward "full political participation by all citizens of South Africa," and confirmed later that "one person, one vote" was a fair translation of his demand. This is abhorrent to most white South Africans.

Within a month of his inauguration, President Carter was reminded of the importance that some members of Congress were beginning to attach to the problem of assuring the nation an adequate supply of critical and strategic materials. He received a letter signed by 43 members of the House of Representatives expressing concern with regard to faltering domestic production of some metals and the growing need for a special minerals advisor in the office of the president. Carter responded by initiating a cabinet-level Nonfuel Minerals Policy Review under the chairmanship of the secretary of the interior. The first of the "serious concerns" assigned by the president for the study was "whether the trends toward international interdependence and the politicization of certain mineral markets are increasing U.S. vulnerability to foreign supply curtailments and price manipulations."

The panel proceeded with more deliberation than speed to hear 42 witnesses, consume 13,000 person-days of work, spend $3.5 million, and produce a report that failed to come to grips with the problem it was assigned to address. The report was a severe disappointment to many of those most concerned with the problem of mineral supply. The appointment of the Nonfuel Minerals Policy Review panel represented the Carter Administration's principal gesture toward the solution of a problem that was clearly causing growing concern elsewhere in the nation.

At the other end of Pennsylvania Avenue, the Congress itself was giving off conflicting and confusing signals. The Senate Foreign Relations Committee, presided over by Senator Frank Church of Idaho, included a subcommittee on Africa headed by Senator George McGovern of South Dakota. During the period of the Carter Administration, the Africa subcommittee produced two reports of note. One, authored largely by Senator McGovern and entitled *Impressions of Southern Africa*, recommended the institution of sanctions against South Africa until that government accepted a U.N. plan for the independence of Namibia, a territory ruled by South Africa since 1920 under a League of Nations mandate. Senator McGovern's report urged continued U.S. pressure "for specific statutory and institutional changes to avoid a bloody race war in Southern Africa."[5] The report further recommended U.S. recognition for the Marxist-run, Cuban-supported regime in Angola.

Later, in September 1980, the Africa subcommittee released a report prepared at its direction by the Congressional Research Service, aimed at downplaying the importance of South Africa as a mineral supplier to the U.S. "The key conclusion of this report," said the text, ". . . is that South African minerals are of significant, but not critical, importance to the West."[6]

On the other side of Capitol Hill, some of the key committees of the House took a substantially contrary view. Congressman Jim Santini of Nevada, chairman of the Mines and Mining subcommittee, wrote a strong rejoinder to the Senate Foreign Relation Committee view on South Africa's significance as a mineral supplier.

Earlier, Congressman Santini had led a delegation from his sub-committee and staff on a tour of Zaire, Zimbabwe (the new name for the former nation of Rhodesia) and South Africa. In its report, the Santini subcommittee gave special note to U.S. relations with South Africa:

America . . . has a vital interest in the survival of South Africa as a Western ally. . . .

There can be little question but that changes in past and some present U.S. policies in dealing with South Africa must take place, both for the peaceful survival of that Nation as well as for basic human concerns. But, past U.S. approaches and policies in dealing with South Africa have been manifestly self-defeating and unsuccessful. If we hope to be a positive force in inducing change, this is hardly to be accomplished by cutting off communications, the U.S. policy in South Africa that has managed to result in the worst of all possible postures. . . .

First, diplomatic communication must be opened with South African political leaders; to ignore the existing political structure accomplishes nothing, as past failure has proved. . . .

The United States should re-establish respectful lines of communication with South African Government and business leaders. Actions which verge on interference by U.S. Government officials in South African domestic politics and policies no matter how highly motivated or well intended, are counterproductive. . . .

Given the presence of South African mining operations at the cutting edge of racial progress in that country, and given the extraordinary concentration in their Nation of much of the world resources of many vital mineral products that are important to the survival of the West, the subcommittee takes the position that the U.S. Government should exhibit encouragement and interest in South Africa's undertakings and in their efforts—and that threats of international sanctions against South Africa should be opposed. Closer ties with the South African mineral industries at a time of growing cartelization by mineral suppliers cannot but help America's long term interests and needs.[7]

Another House group, the Committee on Armed Services, headed by Congressman Melvin Price of Illinois, also expressed official concern for policies indirectly bearing on relations with Southern Africa and with South Africa. A committee task force known as the Defense Industrial Base Panel, headed by Congressman Richard

Ichord of Missouri, undertook a detailed examination of the nation's defense-preparedness posture from the standpoint of its industrial base and its access to strategic materials, and concluded in a report released in December 1980:

> A shortage of critical materials, combined with a resulting depen-
> dence on uncertain foreign sources for these materials, is endan-
> gering the very foundation of our defense capabilities. These
> shortages are a monumental challenge to the Congress, the De-
> partment of Defense, the defense industry and the civilian
> economy.[8]

Further, the panel noted:

> Much of the world's production and reserves of a number of our
> critical materials are located in two areas of the world: Siberia and
> Southern Africa. These two areas contain 99 percent of the world's
> manganese ore; 97 percent of the world's vanadium; 96 percent of
> the world's chrome; 87 percent of the world's diamonds; 60 per-
> cent of the world's vermiculite; and 50 percent of the world's
> fluorspar, iron ore, asbestos, and uranium. Zaire and Zambia now
> provide 65 percent of the world's cobalt.[9]

At a minimum, these expressions of congressional concern suggest the development of a growing political consensus looking toward the acceptance of solutions, even if those solutions involve major government expenditures and some adjustment of foreign and domestic policies that have prevailed in recent years.

It is perhaps significant that an election that brought to power the Reagan Administration with its pledged determination to attack the problem of minerals dependency also brought defeat to senators McGovern and Church, who seemingly regarded social reform as America's prime foreign policy objective in Africa. The same election returned to office congressmen Santini, Price and Ichord, who assumed leadership in seeking solutions to the minerals problems.

A FRESH APPROACH IN AFRICA

The early months of the Reagan Administration produced many signs of an evolving U.S. policy in Southern Africa. One of the thorniest issues confronting the U.S. in the area was the question of independence for Namibia. In its efforts, the U.S. worked with a

Western contact group that included Britain, France, West Germany and Canada to find a solution satisfactory to South Africa as well as to the surrounding black nations that were pressing for Namibian independence.

In this and other issues, the U.S. appeared to have decided that it could accomplish more by working with South Africa than by shouting at it. The reality was that no solution to the Namibian problem could be reached without the cooperation of South Africa.

To serve as its top Africa hand, assistant secretary of state for African affairs, the Reagan Administration selected Chester Crocker, a respected expert on the region. As a professor at Georgetown University and director of African studies at Georgetown's Center for Strategic and International Studies, Crocker had made a career studying and writing about African affairs; he knew the region and many of its leaders and had an understanding of its political complexities. This placed him in contrast with many of his predecessors, most of whom had been either outright political appointees or professional diplomats selected for reasons other than their expertise on Africa. Mr. Crocker had also served in the early 1970s on the staff of the National Security Council.

In a major review of African policy delivered before an American Legion gathering in Honolulu, Mr. Crocker spelled out some of the realities of U.S. relations with the African nations: "The United States has no desire nor, for that matter, any mandate, to act as the policeman of Africa." Yet, he added, "U.S. and Western interests can only be advanced by serious and determined U.S. leadership aimed at strengthening [Southern Africa's] security and backing its development potential. We have defined a new regional strategy, responsive to our national security, economic-commercial, and political interests."

As for relations with Pretoria, Mr. Crocker said:

> In South Africa, the region's dominant country, it is not our task to choose between black and white. In this rich land of talented and diverse peoples, important Western economic, strategic, moral and political interests are at stake. We must avoid action that aggravates the awesome challenges facing South Africans of all races. The Reagan Administration has no intention of destabilizing South Africa in order to curry favor elsewhere. Neither will we align ourselves with apartheid policies that are abhorrent to our own multi-

racial democracy. South Africa is an integral and important element of the global economic system, and it plays a significant economic role in its own region. We will not support the severing of those ties. It does not serve our interests to walk away from South Africa any more than it does to play down the seriousness of domestic and regional problems it faces.[10]

U.S. BUSINESS AND SOUTH AFRICA

Whatever the varying state of relations between the governments in Pretoria and Washington, the government of South Africa made clear its welcome to foreign investors, including Americans. The government provided a favorable rate of exchange on rand acquired for investment in South Africa; it pursued tax policies benign to foreign-owned businesses, maintained an efficient infrastructure of rail, highway, electric power and communication services, and provided for the repatriation of profits, though it enforced certain regulations on the repatriation of capital. American investment in South Africa continued to increase over the decade, particularly in the capital-intensive fields of manufacturing and the recovery and processing of minerals.

By 1980 American investment in South Africa was about $4 billion; this was only about 4 percent of the total business investment in South Africa, but it constituted a highly visible sector of the economy. Ford and General Motors together built about one-third of South Africa's automobiles. Mobil and Caltex were major oil importers and distributors. IBM was the biggest presence in computers. Union Carbide, Phelps Dodge, Amax and Newmont Mining all had significant operations in minerals.

As the Carter-era criticism of South Africa grew in the U.S., many of these companies and others came under pressure from their stockholders and from political activist organizations to curtail or eliminate their business operations in South Africa. One device frequently used to bring pressure on corporate managements was the presentation of stockholder resolutions calling upon management to restrict or end its operations in South Africa.

Possibly the most active of the pressure groups working for disinvestment was the American Friends Service Committee, but a large number of foundations, universities and other nonprofit groups felt impelled to examine their investment policies in the light of a stated reluctance to take profits from a system based upon apartheid practices. Harvard University appointed a special committee of students, faculty and alumni to recommend corporate voting policies to the managers of the university's substantial endowment fund.

Harvard's eventual decision was not to recommend a policy of disinvestment to the corporations in which it held stock, but rather to urge the companies to engage in "responsible" corporate behavior with regard to employment and working practices in South Africa. A Harvard spokesman explained the university's view: "We are agnostic on the issue of withdrawal. We have been unable to determine whether the cause for black South Africa would be advanced by the withdrawal of U.S. industry or advanced by the maintenance of industry there."

The view of industry itself was much less ambivalent, and investment and trade continued to expand. Some of the American corporations, led by General Motors, adopted the Sullivan Principles, a code of employment conduct drafted by the Reverend Leon Sullivan, a member of the G.M. board, setting forth standards for the hiring and employment of black and white South Africans in the fairest possible manner within the constraints of South African law.

This approach was not too different from the general line recommended by Harry Oppenheimer, long-time chairman of the multinational mining giant Anglo American Corporation of South Africa. He has argued that for economic rather than political reasons, the growth of a modern free-enterprise economy will force change upon South Africa's social and political structure and gradually undermine apartheid.

An Anglo American executive, Dennis Etheredge, who in 1980 was president of the South Africa Chamber of Mines, expanded upon this theme in an interview with a visiting journalist. "I certainly accept and understand that a country like ours needs continuing pressure on it to change," he said. "In any country there is an inherent resistance to change. Attitudes are very hard to change, particularly when they are as ingrained as they are among the whites in this country, and go back not a generation but hundreds of years. So left to ourselves, we won't move particularly fast. Therefore pressure upon us, intelligent pressure, I believe must help."

The future direction of the National party government headed by Prime Minister Pieter W. Botha is unclear. Soon after Botha succeeded the hard-lining John Vorster in 1978, he acted in ways that appeared to place him closer to the more liberal (*verligte*—literally, "enlightened") wing of his party, as opposed to the conservative (*verkrampte*—"cramped") wing. The new prime minister appointed a number of commissions to recommend legislative reform, and greeted their recommendations with what sounded like measured approval. He appointed a president's council of white, Coloured (mixed race) and Asian members to advise the government on constitutional change. The appointment of nonwhites to this kind of body was seen as a progressive step, but the absence of any representatives from the black population weakened the council's support and led black leaders to decline to serve even as unofficial advisors.

Those who thought they saw in Mr. Botha the most progressive of the National party prime ministers were doomed to disappointment. Confronted with criticism from his party's conservatives, he called an election and campaigned largely on a platform of adherence to traditional National party values. Even so, a small party called the Herstigte (purified) National party, even more conservative on racial issues than the ruling Nationalists, siphoned off nearly 14 percent of the popular vote. With losses also to the Liberal Progressive Federal party, Mr. Botha's Nationalists saw their overall vote slip to 56 percent, down from 65 percent in 1977.

All of this suggests that South Africa under Mr. Botha will move only slowly toward social reform, regardless of pressures from the thin ranks of South African liberals, from the U.S. or from other Western nations.

This, in turn, suggests that South African blacks and their friends in the black nations of Southern Africa may despair of significant reform from the ruling Nationalists, and conclude that revolutionary violence is the only path to change in South Africa. The U.S. has a powerful interest in averting a violent revolution in South Africa, and to that end seeks to remain on speaking terms with both the entrenched rulers of South Africa and those who work for change, violent or nonviolent.

3

Subcontinental Chaos in Southern Africa

The Southern African subcontinent from Zaire to the Cape of Good Hope contains what is almost surely the world's greatest concentration of nonfuel strategic minerals and the largest known reserves of the most critical—chromium, manganese, cobalt and the platinum metals. Southern African mines produce 18 of the 22 minerals judged most critical to the U.S. economy, as well as gold and gem diamonds, which are economically important if not supercritical.

In an orderly and rational world, this region, with its need for capital, jobs, machinery and know-how should be a perfect trading partner for the mineral-consuming technologically advanced economies of the U.S., Western Europe and Japan. But in the real world, the picture is flawed. Most of the nations of Southern Africa, with the notable exception of the Republic of South Africa, lack the infrastructure, the railroads, highways, communications and power supply to sustain an expanding mining and mineral processing industry, and they are increasingly suspicious of foreign interests who wish to exploit their resources.

Since the period of European colonial rule effectively ended for most of these countries in the 1960s, the young nations have struggled to work out their own destinies. Disorders ranging from tribal struggles to modern warfare have cost lives, time and resources. In many areas, public safety and the quality of public services have eroded in the last two decades.

The former colonial rulers have been limited in what they could do to preserve a semblance of international order in postcolonial Africa. British statesmanship with an assist from the U.S. helped to end the black-white civil war in Rhodesia and launch the new black-ruled Zimbabwe as a viable nation. French diplomacy and military power have served to unseat despots and preserve the orderly processes of international law in Francophone Africa. The socialist government of François Mitterand has not clearly signaled its intentions

U.S. NET IMPORT RELIANCE OF SELECTED MINERALS AND METALS AS A PERCENT OF CONSUMPTION IN 1981 [1]

MINERALS AND METALS [2]	NET IMPORT RELIANCE* AS A PERCENT OF APPARENT CONSUMPTION**	MAJOR FOREIGN SOURCES [3] (1977-1980)
COLUMBIUM	100	BRAZIL, CANADA, THAILAND
DIAMOND (industrial stones)	100	IRELAND, REP. OF SOUTH AFRICA, BELG.-LUX., U.K.
GRAPHITE (natural)	100	MEXICO, REP. OF KOREA, MADAGASCAR, U.S.S.R.
MICA (sheet)	100	INDIA, BRAZIL, MADAGASCAR
STRONTIUM	100	MEXICO
MANGANESE	98	REP. OF SOUTH AFRICA, GABON, FRANCE, BRAZIL
BAUXITE & ALUMINA	94	JAMAICA, AUSTRALIA, GUINEA, SURINAME
COBALT	91	ZAIRE, BELG.-LUX., ZAMBIA, FINLAND
TANTALUM	91	THAILAND, CANADA, MALAYSIA, BRAZIL
CHROMIUM	90	REP. OF SOUTH AFRICA, PHILIPPINES, U.S.S.R., FINLAND
FLUORSPAR	85	MEXICO, REP. OF SOUTH AFRICA, SPAIN, ITALY
PLATINUM—GROUP METALS	85	REP. OF SOUTH AFRICA, U.S.S.R., U.K.
ASBESTOS	80	CANADA, REP. OF SOUTH AFRICA
TIN	80	MALAYSIA, THAILAND, BOLIVIA, INDONESIA
NICKEL	72	CANADA, NORWAY, BOTSWANA, AUSTRALIA
POTASH	68	CANADA, ISRAEL
ZINC	67	CANADA, MEXICO, SPAIN, AUSTRALIA
CADMIUM	63	CANADA, AUSTRALIA, MEXICO, BELG.-LUX.
TUNGSTEN	52	CANADA, BOLIVIA, MAINLAND CHINA, THAILAND
ANTIMONY	51	REP. OF SOUTH AFRICA, BOLIVIA, MAINLAND CHINA, MEXICO
SILVER	50	CANADA, MEXICO, PERU, U.K.
SELENIUM	49	CANADA, JAPAN, YUGOSLAVIA
BARIUM	43	PERU, MAINLAND CHINA, IRELAND, MOROCCO, CHILE
TITANIUM (ilmenite)	43	AUSTRALIA, CANADA, REP. OF SOUTH AFRICA
VANADIUM	42	REP. OF SOUTH AFRICA, CHILE, CANADA
MERCURY	39	SPAIN, ALGERIA, JAPAN, ITALY
GYPSUM	37	CANADA, MEXICO, JAMAICA
IRON ORE	28	CANADA, VENEZUELA, BRAZIL, LIBERIA
IRON & STEEL	14	JAPAN, EUROPE, CANADA
LEAD	10	CANADA, MEXICO, PERU
GOLD	7	CANADA, U.S.S.R., SWITZERLAND
SULFUR	7	CANADA, MEXICO
COPPER	5	CHILE, CANADA, PERU, ZAMBIA

*NET IMPORT RELIANCE = IMPORTS-EXPORTS
+ADJUSTMENTS FOR GOV'T AND INDUSTRY STOCK CHANGES.

**APPARENT CONSUMPTION = U.S. PRIMARY
+SECONDARY PRODUCTION + NET IMPORT RELIANCE.

[1] JANUARY 20, 1982 (ESTIMATE).

[2] SUBSTANTIAL QUANTITIES ARE IMPORTED FOR RUTILE, RHENIUM AND ZIRCON. DATA WITHHELD TO AVOID DISCLOSING COMPANY PROPRIETARY DATA.

[3] SOURCES SHOWN ARE POINTS OF SHIPMENT TO THE U.S. AND ARE NOT NECESSARILY THE INITIAL SOURCES OF THE MATERIAL.

BUREAU OF MINES, U.S. DEPARTMENT OF THE INTERIOR
(import-export data from Bureau of the Census)

in this regard, but it has invited a guerrilla movement from Namibia to open a representative office in Paris.

The region's future is filled with other imponderables. Now that the Soviet Union has engineered the creation of friendly regimes in Angola and Mozambique, will it use those two nations as a base to expand its influence in the region? Will Marxist Angola eventually dominate its resource-rich, people-poor neighbor Namibia if and when South Africa is forced to vacate its mandate there? Will nations under Soviet domination or Soviet threat continue to supply their strategic raw materials to the West in an international crisis?

Yet another question troubling Western strategists is the future of the Cape sea route, through which a stream of tanker-borne oil flows from the Middle East to Western Europe and the U.S. Clearly, an unfriendly power with naval strength based in Southern Africa could gravely threaten the security of the sea route. Will the Soviet Union do so? Some strategists tend to dismiss this threat on the grounds that in an all-out conflict with the West the Soviets would not choose a point of confrontation so far from its own bases of power. Others are not so sure. The question, like so many others involving this region, will remain unanswered until events unfold.

Complicating the regional politics of Southern Africa are national rivalries such as those between Zaire and Angola, Mozambique and Malawi, and all the black nations collectively against white-ruled South Africa. Southern Africa is a resource-rich, politically unstable region; it is not an area on which the West would choose to depend for many of its most vital raw materials. But those are the cards that nature and international politics have dealt, and the West will have to play them.

Here are some of the players in this Southern Africa drama.

BOTSWANA

Formerly the British protectorate of Bechuanaland, Botswana is a vast empty stretch of landlocked real estate, half again the size of California with a population smaller than San Diego's. Once a major cattle-raising region, Botswana is still an exporter of beef and an importer of grain, refined oil and technology from South Africa.

Mining is of growing importance in Botswana, and was the fastest growing sector of the economy in the late 1970s, providing a major portion of the nation's export earnings and a substantial share of the government's revenues. By 1979 Botswana had become the world's fourth largest producer of diamonds, and its share of the world diamond market was growing as new discoveries were opened. Production of copper and nickel was also growing, largely because of development of high-grade ores in the Selebi-Pikwe area. Amax Corporation, the American multinational mining company, shares ownership in the mines along with Anglo American of South Africa, the government of Botswana and some private shareholders. Amax held a contract to process copper-nickel matte from the mines at its refinery in Port Nickel, Louisiana, and to resell a portion of the refined metal to buyers in West Germany. Some cobalt is also recovered from the Botswana ores.

The U.S. Bureau of Mines reports that exploration for coal, uranium, asbestos and base metals is under way in various parts of the country. An airborne geophysical survey conducted by the Canadian International Development Agency and the Botswana Geological Survey indicated a positive potential for many minerals in the Kalahari sands, which cover nearly 80 percent of the country. The Botswana government, which encourages foreign investment, has licensed Falconbridge Mines of Canada to explore for precious stones, copper, nickel, gold, silver and radioactive minerals. An area of southwestern Botswana was judged to hold potential for petroleum exploration as well.

Like other nations in Southern Africa, Botswana is torn between official opposition to South Africa's racial policies and a very practical need for economic cooperation with the dominant power of the region. The Rhodesian–South Africa rail line that passes through eastern Botswana is the nation's lifeline to the outside world. Botswana is linked, along with Lesotho, Swaziland and Namibia, to South Africa through the Southern Africa Customs Union. Many South Africans are employed as bureaucrats and technicians up to the level of permanent undersecretary in the Botswana government.

Pretoria has charged that Botswana allows South African exile groups to operate with impunity from its territory. This is probably true, in part because the government of Botswana lacks the military forces to police effectively all of its thinly populated territory.

ZAMBIA

Zambia, which was known as Northern Rhodesia before gaining its independence from Britain in 1964, is a landlocked country with immense resources in copper and cobalt, and some production of gold, silver, lead and zinc. As a copper producer, it ranks first in Africa, fifth in the world; its cobalt production is exceeded only by that of Zaire.

The mining industry provides some 90 percent of Zambia's foreign exchange; copper production alone accounted for 27 percent of its gross domestic product in 1978. Because jobs in the copper mines are among the best-paying available to uneducated workers and provide access to bright lights and urban life, they have lured away from the rural regions many young men who would otherwise work Zambia's once flourishing but now languishing farms. One result is that Zambia has become an importer of tropical fruits from Zimbabwe and grain from South Africa.

Zambia faces major problems in moving its copper to world markets. The Chinese-built Tazara railroad, completed in 1975, was intended to link the Zambian copper belt with the Tanzanian port of Dar es Salaam, but it has never lived up to the expectations held for it. The line has been plagued with washouts of rails and bridges and by inadequate maintenance that led to frequent derailments.

In 1978 Zambia's president, Kenneth Kaunda, announced the reopening of the southern rail route through Rhodesia (now Zimbabwe) to South African ports, to expedite the shipment of copper and the import of food and fertilizer from South Africa. The South African railways lent Zambia four locomotives to help in the movement of rail freight within Zambia. This was one indication of the anomalous relations that exist between Zambia and South Africa.

On the level of day-to-day commerce, relations work smoothly. Many South African enterprises do business in Zambia, and South Africa's Anglo American Corporation is a major presence in Zambian mining. Harry Oppenheimer, chairman of Anglo American, reportedly has a close and amicable relationship with President Kaunda. So many South African mining executives and businessmen live and work in Lusaka that for many years two schools in the capital were taught in Afrikaans so the students would be qualified to enter high school when they returned home to South Africa.

On the other hand, Kaunda is one of the more outspoken African critics of South Africa's racial policies, and the South African government charges that he shelters guerrillas who stage raids through Botswana into Namibia and South Africa. In 1981, Zambia was one of the sponsors of a resolution adopted in the United Nations General Assembly calling upon all states to "cease forthwith, individually and collectively, all dealings with South Africa in order to totally isolate it politically, economically, militarily and culturally."

It has not escaped the world's attention that if such sanctions were actually to be observed, one of the first to suffer would be Zambia.

ZAIRE

The Republic of Zaire, located in the south-central region of Africa, with a slim strip of territory extending to the Atlantic Ocean, occupies an expanse of rain forest and mountainous upland about equal in area to the United States east of the Mississippi. Its 28 million inhabitants make it the third most populous of the black African states, after Nigeria and Ethiopia.

Formerly known as the Belgian Congo, for many years until 1908 it was the personal property of King Leopold II of Belgium. The Congo negotiated its independence from Belgium in 1960 and immediately fell into a period of civil conflict as rival forces fought for control of the new government. The first elected prime minister, Patrice Lumumba, was murdered, and so, probably, was one of his successors in power, the conservative Moise Tshombe. In 1965, Lieutenant General Joseph Mobutu seized power with the backing of the army, and established a military-based regime that has withstood various challenges to its authority, including three bloody insurrections in the southeastern region where most of the nation's mineral resources are located. In 1971 the president changed his name to Mobutu Sese Seko and renamed the nation Zaire; later he decreed the Africanization of most other place names. Many Zairians with Christian names also found it advisable to assume African names. The mineral-rich province of the southeast became Shaba.

A *Report on Zaire* published in 1978 by the Center for Strategic and International Studies observed:

> Mobutu has demonstrated on numerous occasions considerable political and survival skills. This domestic political skill is only matched by his skill not at managing the economy, but at managing the international lending institutions that have kept his economy afloat. He has pulled his country back from the abyss of default on international debts more than once. Each time Mobutu has promised reform of administrative structures and fiscal practices. Each time new financing has been forthcoming and the crisis of the moment has faded.[1]

In the late 1970s the mineral industry of Zaire generated 60 percent of the nation's foreign exchange and led the world in the production of cobalt and industrial diamonds. Zaire is also a major producer of copper, increasing its output in 1980 by 15 percent over 1979 despite relatively weak prices; it also produces significant amounts of zinc and uranium, some tin, tungsten, gold, silver, cadmium and columbium-tantalum. It is an interesting historical footnote that the Belgian Congo was the source for the uranium from which the first U.S. atom bombs were made. Edgar Sengier, then president of Union Minière, thoughtfully shipped 1,000 tons of ore and stored it in a warehouse in New York and in due course made it available to the Manhattan Project.[2]

Zaire's sales of such high-tonnage products as copper and zinc are limited by the availability of transportation to the outside world. The Benguela railroad from the port of Lobito in Angola to Shaba province was a major transportation artery until the rebellion in Angola in 1975 led to the closing of the line. Because of the activities of antigovernment guerrillas in eastern Angola, it has remained closed except for brief intervals since that time.

Another outlet for Shaba's copper lies by barge route via Kalemie across Lake Tanganyika to the Tazara railroad to the Tanzanian port of Dar es Salaam. But, as mentioned elsewhere, this railroad has proved unreliable, and the port of Dar es Salaam is notorious for its congestion and inefficiency. Shaba's third major outlet lies by rail through Zambia and Zimbabwe to South Africa, and the greater part of Zaire's copper production moves to market by that route.

The U.S. House of Representatives Mines and Mining subcommittee reported after its 1980 tour of Zaire:

> Possessed of an adequate and well-run transportation network before independence, Zaire's present railways, water transport facilities, and road system have deteriorated significantly because of an absence of maintenance, fuel, replacement rolling stock, and spare parts. Lack of good communications (virtually collapsed today in central Zaire and inherently a problem because of language differences) has become a major operational problem in Shaba's mining centers because of unreliable mail delivery and telecommunications.[3]

The single mineral for which Zaire assumes outsize importance to the rest of the world is cobalt, which is recovered along with copper in the mineralized belt that runs for more than 300 kilometers in Zaire and continues into Zambia. Zaire regularly produces more than 50 percent of all the cobalt mined in the world and well over 60 percent of the cobalt consumed in the U.S. and Western Europe. That is why an otherwise minor guerrilla raid in May 1978 sent shock waves through the industrialized world.

The invading force consisted of about 3,000 men of the Marxist-leaning Congo National Liberation Front, based in Angola and believed to have been trained by Cuban mercenaries in Angola. The guerrillas passed through Zambian territory, and on May 13, 1978 arrived in the mining center of Kolwezi in Shaba, where they proceeded to take over the town and order the closing of the mines.

While the army of Zaire serves to keep the government in power in Kinshasa and formerly was notorious for brutalizing civilians, it does not control all of Zaire's outlying regions, and it offered no immediate resistance to the invaders from Angola, who set about working their will on Zairians and Europeans alike. White women were herded to the hotel Impala and forced to dance on a small stage before being raped and shot. Altogether, 93 whites and some 750 Africans were killed in the invasion.[4]

President Mobutu sent a call for help to France's President Valéry Giscard d'Estaing, and the French took the lead in organizing a rescue force of French Foreign Legionnaires and Moroccan and Zairian troops. The soldiers were flown to the scene in U.S. military aircraft, and they promptly drove the invaders back across the border toward Angola.

The guerrillas caused comparatively little damage to the mines during the six days they were in Shaba. The vulnerability of the mines was aptly demonstrated, however. Power for the mine pumps for the Kamoto underground workings was cut off, and the flooding that resulted delayed mining operations for 30 days. Damage was less in the open pits, but it took the mines 50 days to return to normal operations. Production loss was estimated at $28 million.

The invasion had far-reaching effects in the world metal markets. It was widely reported that just prior to the invasion, Soviet purchasing agents had been actively buying up available supplies of cobalt at the preinvasion price of $6.85 a pound. After the invasion, the producer price of cobalt rose to $12.50 a pound in July and to $25 a pound by February, 1979, as buyers rushed to stockpile metal in anticipation of a possible shortage. Spot sales of cobalt were made at prices as high as $49 a pound in November 1978 before the price settled back to around $42 a pound by May 1979.

With a burgeoning world demand at those prices, Zairian producers could affort to bypass the time-consuming rail routes by airlifting cobalt to world markets. The government mining company, GECAMINES, shipped 85 percent of its cobalt by air in 1979 and 100 percent in 1980, reportedly at a cost of $1.50 per kilogram.

The invasion and loss of life had another long-term impact on Zaire's mining industry. Increasingly, European executives, engineers and skilled technicians were reluctant to expose themselves and their families to the risk of further military attacks, and they drifted away from the mines. This vastly increased the difficulties of the mining companies in maintaining the complex mining machinery, and in planning future operations.

Other problems were more obvious to the House Mines and Mining subcommittee: "Internally, years of serious government neglect by failing to plow back sufficient mining revenues had decreased operating efficiency, thus increasing costs." Further, the subcommittee found: "The overwhelming causes [of inefficiency] are economic mismanagement and widespread political corruption, which President Mobutu has personally labeled 'Zairian sickness.'"[5]

A formidable combination of economic and political problems has hindered the further development of Zaire's resources by foreign investors. In 1970 a company called Société Minière de Tenke-Fungurume, a consortium of British, French, Japanese and American interests and the Zairian government, obtained a concession to develop a large and well-defined copper-cobalt deposit in Shaba province near Kolwezi. The lifeline of the operation was to be the Benguela railroad, running from the Angolan port of Lobito to Shaba; this line was to bring in mining machinery and diesel fuel and eventually to haul out metal and concentrates. The closing of the Benguela railroad in 1975 was a severe blow to the consortium's plans, but work continued.

In part because of the political environment in Zaire, in part because of rising development costs and falling copper prices, the project's backers had to call off their plans in 1977; they had spent $280 million on development and machinery and estimated they would need another $500 million to complete the mining and refining complex—well above the cost estimates of $500 million all told that seemed reasonable in 1974. The major American participant, a subsidiary of Standard Oil of Indiana, sold its 28 percent interest to the French Bureau de Recherches Géologiques et Minières which then became the dominant member with 34.4 percent ownership. President Mobutu reportedly is eager for the consortium to proceed with the development of the property, but in 1982 the project seemed very far from completion.

ZIMBABWE

In 1980 the nation of Rhodesia, named for that most imperial of Britons, Cecil Rhodes, won its independence. It assumed its new African name of Zimbabwe and elected a constitutional government. Its new leader, Robert Mugabe, evolved into a conciliatory international statesman, capable of impressing skeptical foreign leaders with his reasonableness, his ability, and his desire to live within the constraints of international law.

In Washington and other Western capitals, he sought and gained commitments for economic aid, and at home he appeared to establish harmonious relations with his former allies and rivals. For a time, white Rhodesians who had regarded his election as the worst possible outcome of the 1980 voting were reassured. As the nation got back to work under its new government after its long civil war, its gross national product showed encouraging gains in 1980 and 1981.

Zimbabwe, roughly the size of Montana, is well endowed with fertile lands, a climate favorable for agriculture and a subsoil rich in highly salable minerals: chromite, the most important, as well as gold, asbestos, nickel, copper, coal, tin, tantalum. Altogether, more than 20 minerals are produced commercially. Although Zimbabwe has no production in platinum metals, it is reported to hold substantial reserves in those rare ores.

Soon after winning election, Mugabe appealed to the nation's whites to remain in Zimbabwe and help him build a prosperous multiracial society. Their skills were urgently needed to keep the nation's mines and farms and its rail system working. For a time white emigration, which became a flood during the civil war, slowed to a trickle. But pressures rose from blacks who had won the revolution and were impatient to collect the spoils in the form of lands and properties formerly controlled by whites. While Mugabe resisted wholesale nationalization of white properties, his government increased taxes and estate levies and cut back on privileges that whites had long enjoyed. The response of an increasing number of whites, especially younger workers with families, was to head for the borders, leaving behind older white workers who would soon be terminating their careers.

Other government measures, planned or enacted, caused concern to foreign businessmen still in Zimbabwe. While Mugabe assured these executives that his government valued their contribution to Zimbabwe's present and future prosperity, his policies were increasing the difficulties of doing business in Zimbabwe. Basic wage costs and the cost of hauling ores rose sharply after independence. Further, the government gave notice of its intention to assume control of the international marketing of 40 minerals other than gold (which was already under rigid government marketing controls). Pending the creation of the new marketing boards and the appointment of the officials who would run them, Western businessmen could not be sure just how the new system would work, but many were apprehensive.

The government maintained that the new measures were necessary to halt the practice by Zimbabwean subsidiaries of selling their minerals to parent companies at less than world market prices, with loss of tax revenue to Zimbabwe. For their part, mining executives were equally concerned that the government boards might sell or withhold minerals more in response to political needs and the changing demands for foreign exchange than for more basic economic and marketing considerations. It was widely reported in Zimbabwe that two Swedish mining companies had held up plans to open new chrome mining and smelting operations in Zimbabwe at least until the new ground rules were clarified.

Further, the government gave notice of its intention to increase Zimbabwean equity ownership of major industries, which had been largely controlled by foreign companies. To some foreign investors this sounded like progressive nationalization, with the increasing costs and inefficiencies that government control implied.

Some U.S. critics of South Africa have proposed that the West should reduce its dependence upon South African chrome by relying more heavily upon sources in Zimbabwe, but to a U.S. Bureau of Mines expert, Ebraham Shekarchi, this is not a practical alternative. In a report published in 1981,[6] Mr. Shekarchi estimated that Zimbabwe could maintain production of chromite and the more highly refined ferrochrome, which now absorbs 75 percent of Zimbabwe's chromite production, at something like its 1980 rate for many years. But to increase substantially its rate of production would be very difficult because of limitations on electric power supply, metallurgical coal and skilled manpower. Mr. Shekarchi concluded:

> With its annual production of roughly half a million tons, Zimbabwe's chrome output is only one-sixth that of South Africa and between one-fifth and one-fourth that of the Soviet Union. Considering this relatively modest role, Zimbabwe would not be able to make much of a contribution to relieving any shortage caused by an interruption in deliveries from South Africa to the West. Since the Soviet Union provides only one-fourth of its output to the West, Zimbabwe would have to double its production to make up this loss.

Mugabe's relations with South Africa remain tenuous. While he freely admits his country's economic dependence upon South Africa for many goods and services, he refused to enter into political or diplomatic relations with Pretoria. In April 1981 South Africa withdrew 25 diesel locomotives that it had leased to Zimbabwe's railways. This key loss, combined with the ongoing loss of skilled white workers, was a severe setback to the national rail system and in turn to the nation's export trade, which depends heavily upon rail transport. Even so, some 80 percent of Zimbabwe's exports continued to move through South Africa.

Zimbabwe expected to take delivery by 1982 on the first of 60 new diesel locomotives ordered in the U.S. and Canada with financial aid from Kuwait. Even before the new locomotives arrived, the railways began to hire skilled mechanics and craftsmen from India. A white official told a *New York Times* correspondent: "Ultimately you are going to have to maintain the country with Indians, or it is going to go down the drain."[7]

In mid-1982, it was too soon to know which of the conflicting political and economic forces would guide the government of Robert Mugabe: the economic imperative to encourage foreign investment for rapid development and creation of jobs, or the political imperative to nationalize, tax and control. It was equally unclear whether Mugabe would join the other black leaders of the region in a militant hostility to South Africa, or seek pragmatic ways to coexist. The conflict, in fact, was rather graphically illustrated in Zimbabwe's newly designed coat of arms. It showed a hoe, a Soviet-designed AK-47 assault rifle and the motto "Unity, freedom, work."

NAMIBIA

Namibia, or South West Africa, to use its older name, is a vast stretch of largely barren land two-thirds the size of South Africa but with only 1 million inhabitants, 10 percent of them white. A German colony before World War I, it was placed under control of South Africa by a League of Nations mandate in 1920, and it has been administered by South Africa since that time. Namibia has been the focus of an angry international debate between South Africa and much of black Africa, in particular the so-called frontline states of Angola, Botswana, Mozambique, Tanzania, Zimbabwe and Zambia.

In the 1960s the African states charged that South Africa imposed apartheid in South West Africa, exploited its resources and built military bases there. They launched a move to gain self-government for the territory. In 1968 the United Nations General Assembly began referring to the territory by its African name of Namibia, and in 1970 the General Assembly passed a resolution condemning South Africa for retaining "illegal" control of the area. The resolution called upon South Africa to begin a transition to self-government for Namibia.

In a 1977 referendum, white voters of Namibia endorsed a plan for a multiracial government as a step toward independence. However, the South West Africa Peoples Organization, the largest of the militant groups seeking independence for Namibia, rejected the results of the referendum, and with the political support of Marxist Angola and arms from the Eastern Bloc stepped up a guerrilla war against the South African regime. That guerrilla war has continued to 1982 and seems likely to go on until a political settlement is reached.

South Africa has fought back with raids on guerrilla camps in Namibia and across the border in Angola. In late 1981 it launched the largest of these operations to date, sending two columns of troops supported by armor and air power deep into Angola to attack guerrilla bases and destroy radar stations and air defenses protecting the bases. The South Africans reported killing, along with guerrillas, a number of Soviet officers and capturing a Russian warrant officer. While South Africa and Western nations had long known that the Soviets were actively arming and supporting the guerrillas, this was seen as the first proof of Soviet participation in combat operations.

The South Africa raid was followed by adoption of a resolution in the United Nations General Assembly condemning "the illegal occupation of Namibia by South Africa." The U.S. and 24 other countries, mostly Western, abstained from the General Assembly vote, but took the occasion to urge South Africa to open new discussions with the Western Contact group (Britain, France, West Germany, Canada and the U.S.) on eventual independence for Namibia.

The apparent goal of the West was to solve the Namibian dispute in a way that would not place the nation and its large and strategic mineral resources under control of a government dominated by the Marxist SWAPO movement. At the same time, the African frontline states continued to press for a solution that would effectively install SWAPO as the dominant political force in Namibia.

The economy. While some areas of Namibia are suitable for farming and cattle raising, the mineral industry contributes approximately 50 percent of the value of Namibia's gross domestic product. From a strategic viewpoint, the most important of Namibia's mineral products is uranium. Rossing Uranium Ltd., owned by Britain's Rio Tinto Zinc and French and South African interests and managed by Rio Tinto, operates the world's biggest uranium mine. The output of the mine is sold mainly to buyers in Britain, France, Germany and Japan.

Tsumeb Corporation, owned principally by the American companies Amax and Newmont Mining and managed by Newmont, is Namibia's major base metal producer, mining copper, lead and zinc, and recovering some silver, cadmium and arsenic as by-products. Diamond mining is largely the province of Consolidated Diamond Mines, a subsidiary of the De Beers interests of South Africa. Approximately 95 percent of the diamonds recovered are of gem quality, an unusually high proportion. Because of world market conditions, diamond production in Namibia was in a downtrend in the years after 1977.

Exploration for new mineral deposits continued in the late 1970s under the auspices of South African mining companies. Results of an airborne geophysical survey of the northern and eastern regions of the country were placed in an open file with the Geological Survey of South West Africa.

The U.S. Bureau of Mines reports that a consortium of British and South African engineering companies was studying the feasibility of building a trans-Kalahari railroad, from Francistown in northern Botswana to the existing railhead at Gobabis in South West Africa. It seems unlikely that this project will succeed until the political future of Namibia becomes clearer.

ANGOLA

The importance of Angola does not lie in its known mineral resources, which, except for oil and diamonds, are meager. It lies rather in the political role Angola has adopted as an ally of the Soviet Union and host to a Cuban expeditionary force, in its position as a geographical keystone bordering Namibia, Zambia and Zaire, and in its potential as an outlet to the Atlantic for the landlocked states to the east and north.

Ruled by the Portuguese for nearly 400 years, Angola gained independence suddenly in 1975 after a coup d'etat in Lisbon brought to power a new government with no desire to cling to Portugal's African colonies, Angola and Mozambique. Guerrilla activity, which had simmered for years in both countries, boiled up, and when the fighting was over both countries were ruled by former guerrilla leaders with an ideological commitment to Marxism and a debt to the Soviet Union for military aid. In Angola, the principal military power rested with an expeditionary force of about 20,000 Cuban soldiers plus East European advisors, all installed through the direct intervention of the Soviet Union.

In Angola, the principal preindependence movements were:

1. The Popular Movement for the Liberation of Angola (MPLA), led by a physician and poet, Dr. Agostinho Neto. The MPLA drew its internal support from the Mimbundu, the Lunda and the substantial mulatto community, representing all told about one-third of the population of Angola. The external support it drew from the Communist bloc was crucial to subsequent events.

2. The National Front for the Liberation of Angola (FNLA), led by Holden Roberto. Its strength was centered in the north among the Bakongo, who represented about 15 percent of Angola's population, and it had external support from Zaire, where it maintained its oper-

ational headquarters, from the People's Republic of China and from the U.S. Its military arm was staffed in part by Portuguese and some other mercenaries, but the quality of its political and military leadership was poor. As one Western diplomat said later, "Holden Roberto turned out to be pretty much a traditional African expatriate revolutionary, with a lot of rhetoric and very few troops." FNLA fared poorly in battle with the Cuban-aided MPLA forces, and has faded as a center of influence.

3. The National Union for the Total Independence of Angola, led by Jonas Savimbi, a charismatic Western-educated figure with considerable support among the Ovimbundu people in the center and south of Angola. A 1976 study[8] written by Chester Crocker, later assistant secretary of state for African affairs, suggested that with a popular following of 40 to 65 percent of the population, "UNITA could win a majority in a free election, something Angola has never had."

But the civil struggle of 1975 and 1976 was not decided by ballot; it was carried by the overwhelming force of Cuban arms supporting Neto's MPLA. Crocker's *Report on Angola* notes:

> The MPLA offensive resulted from an awesome imbalance of military power: a political-military struggle between fairly evenly matched liberation movements was transformed by the deployment of ten percent of the Cuban army to Angola, armed with the full range of equipment—MIGs, 122 mm rocket launchers, and over 1,000 tanks, armored cars and trucks—used by a modern mechanized army. Not since World War II has such a coalition of external and local troops campaigned on the African continent.[9]

South Africa attempted to influence events by pushing a force of 1,500 men some 500 miles into Angola to take pressure off Jonas Savimbi's UNITA forces. But as the tide turned against Savimbi and his troops, the South African force withdrew, bowing to domestic and international opposition to its presence, and to the difficulty of confronting a large well-armed and well-trained force hundreds of miles from its own bases.

Savimbi and UNITA in turn retreated to the countryside of the south and east of Angola, where they have continued a low-level guerrilla operation that has denied to the government in Luanda full sovereign control of its own territory. UNITA has almost surely received substantial support from South Africa, which is eager to keep the Angolan government off balance, and to inhibit it in its support of the Angolan-based SWAPO. South Africa's military thrust into Angola in late 1981 (see section on Namibia) thus had the dual purpose of applying pressure on Angola and easing SWAPO's pressure on Namibia. Some of the Soviet-made arms captured from SWAPO and Angolan troops in that raid may have been handed over to Savimbi's UNITA forces.

The U.S. has been more an observer than participant in recent events in Angola. In 1976 a U.S. Congress suffering the shock of defeat in Vietnam adopted an amendment prohibiting the executive branch from aiding any guerrilla forces in Angola without the specific approval of the Congress. In 1981 the Reagan Administration asked Congress to repeal that amendment. The Administration professed no desire to involve itself in Angola, but rather said it wanted a free hand to deal with events as they developed. The Senate voted repeal, but the House denied the president's request and the amendment remained in effect.

Soon after his appointment as assistant secretary of state for African affairs, Chester Crocker made a tour of Southern African capitals, including Luanda, where the U.S. has no official relations, in part because of the U.S.'s strong objection to the presence of Cuban troops in Angola. In a policy speech delivered in Honolulu in August, 1981, Mr. Crocker said: "It is unlikely that the struggle between the MPLA government and opposition forces—chiefly UNITA, led by Jonas Savimbi—can be resolved militarily. Cuban troop withdrawal and national reconciliation would be supported by all Angola's neighbors. . . ." The U.S. position in Angola, as in Namibia, is to work for a reconciliation among the warring forces and to work out a sharing of power.

The economy. While Angola is clearly Marxist in political orientation, it has not yet become a classic, monolithic Communist state. Whether it will do so under its new leader, Jose Eduardo dos Santos, who succeeded the late Agostinho Neto in 1979, is one of the key political questions for Southern Africa.

In 1976 Angola became a participant in the Soviet-led Council for Economic Mutual Assistance (COMECON), and in the late 1970s it signed a number of economic aid and cooperation agreements with the Soviet Union and Cuba; other agreements were signed with Yugoslavia, Bulgaria and East Germany, but also with Sweden, and discussions were held with the European Economic Community. Soviet experts were at work exploring Angola's mineral resources and were to make a geological map of Angola.

On the other hand, Western companies, most notably Pittsburgh-based Gulf Oil, were operating in oil-rich Cabinda province, an enclave of Angola separated from the rest of the nation by the sliver of territory where Zaire touches the Atlantic. Gulf alone produced oil at the rate of 93,000 barrels a day in 1981. The oil fields yielded the state more than half of its total revenue and most of its foreign exchange. The U.S. Bureau of Mines reported, "As a result of a new law providing for production sharing and more favorable attitude towards foreign investment, several new petroleum exploration and production contracts were signed in 1979." It is a little ironic that the success and continued operation of the Cabinda oil wells is due in no small part to the military security provided by Cuban troops assigned to the region.

Aside from oil, Angola produces gem and industrial diamonds, and the government has recruited the help of foreign corporations to help it expand production of diamonds to prewar levels. Other mineral production in Angola is minor, but because of its geology, Angola is considered a promising area for further exploration. Whether that exploration and development will be done by East or West is still an unanswered question.

MOZAMBIQUE

Mozambique, like Angola, is a former Portuguese colony that gained independence following Portugal's 1974 coup d'etat. On June 25, 1975 effective power was handed over to a force called the Front for the Liberation of Mozambique (FRELIMO), which had waged a guerrilla war against the Portuguese since 1964. During the long struggle, FRELIMO and its leader, Samora Machel, operated from bases in neighboring Tanzania and received arms, training and political indoctrination from the Soviet Union as well as other Eastern Bloc nations, Cuba and the People's Republic of China. In power, Machel declared his intention to create a Marxist-Leninist state centrally directed by FRELIMO and maintaining close ties with other Communist states. Those, in fact, are the lines along which postcolonial Mozambique has evolved.

The influence of the Soviet Union and the Eastern Bloc has

continued to be strong. Mozambique maintains especially close relations with East Germany, which appears to provide special assistance in the field of internal security. East Germans are reported to have trained and partly staffed President Machel's personal bodyguard, and they are in charge of security at Maputo's international airport. Of Maputo, a South African businessman said: "Not many people go touring there because it can be a little unpleasant spending three hours at the airport while you are stripped naked and searched."

At the political level, relations between Mozambique and South Africa are cold to hostile. Machel loses no opportunity to join public condemnation of South Africa's "racist" regime. For its part, South Africa charges that Mozambique shelters and aids "terrorists," and in particular members of the outlawed African National Congress. From time to time South Africa raids guerrilla camps and staging areas in Mozambique. In 1980 a group of South African soldiers swimming at a beach near the ill-defined border wandered into Mozambique and one South African was killed by Mozambican border guards. South Africa entered a stiff protest, and a few days later two Soviet warships paid a visit to Maputo.

On another level, relations between South Africa and Mozambique are brisk and mutually supportive. South Africa provides food, machinery and a variety of technical services, including those of experts maintaining and improving Maputo's port facilities. In 1977 Maputo handled nearly 12 million tons of export freight, half of it from South Africa, and in 1978 the government of Mozambique negotiated an agreement providing for South Africa to double its exports by 1985. Mozambique borrowed a number of locomotives from South Africa and with the help of South African engineers began to upgrade and improve its railway system, largely to facilitate the movement of minerals from South Africa and Zimbabwe to Indian Ocean ports.

A giant hydroelectric dam on the Zambezi river, the Cabora Bassa, was built largely with South African capital. Started during the Portuguese regime, it was completed shortly before independence, and in 1976 began to supply electricity to the South African power grid, providing eventually about 10 percent of South Africa's power needs and yielding Mozambique about $4 million a month in revenue. Saboteurs, reportedly members of an anti-Machel underground in Mozambique, succeeded in damaging the transmission lines from the dam late in 1980; power supply from the dam has been intermittent since that time.

South African gold mines employ large numbers of laborers from Mozambique and other African nations. In 1980 these migrant workers numbered about 200,000, of whom about 40,000 were from Mozambique. Recruited in their home countries, the workers are transported to South Africa, given physical and mental examinations and trained for several weeks before being assigned to jobs in the mines. Since the workers often come from areas with no common language, as part of the training program the mine managements teach the workers a common, artificial language called Fanagalo, a mixture of tribal tongues, English and Afrikaans. Each worker must absorb enough of this special language to accept instructions and communicate with his supervisors and fellow workers, with whom he may share no other language.

For many of the migrant workers, mine jobs are the best available, and a rare opportunity for wage-paying work in the money economy. Their wages are an important contribution to their families, and remitted wages significantly aid the balance of payments of Mozambique and other countries where the miners are recruited.

Mines and minerals. Mozambique is not a major producer of minerals, through it does mine and sell some copper, some gem and ornamental stones and the highly strategic columbite-tantalite ore. Its resources in the latter minerals are believed to be substantial; its 1980 production was about 8 percent of the world total. Mozambique's greater significance in critical and strategic materials is its function as an outlet to the Indian Ocean for South African and Zimbabwean minerals.

4

Pacific Producers: Mexico, Canada, Australia

Are These Countries Stable for Mining Investment?

BY SIMON HUNT
BROOK HUNT & ASSOCIATES, CONSULTANTS, LONDON

Over the past decade, concern has grown over the long-term availability of certain essential raw materials from some developing countries. There have been three main reasons for this concern. First, many governments of developing countries have evolved unfavorable tax and ownership policies, which have resulted in substantial declines in exploration and mining by overseas companies in those areas. Second, geopolitical and geostrategic developments, particularly in Southern Africa and Central America, have shown how vulnerable the Western world would become if exports of materials like cobalt and chromium were denied to the West. Third, in some countries, like Zambia, there exists a long-term decline in reserves and production of its principal raw-material export, namely copper.

Combined, these factors have produced a number of changes. Governments have been considering the establishment of stockpiles of materials, and the Americans and the French have started to rebuild their stocks. In the private sector, funds are being launched to make long-term portfolio investments in metals. In addition, and equally important, many multinational companies that had historically supported exploration in many Least Developed Countries (LDCs),[1] particularly in Central Africa, have either pulled out or reduced their exposure to a minimum. Meanwhile, multinational companies increased significantly their investments in Canada, Australia and, to a lesser degree, Mexico. These three countries have been generally considered politically stable for mining investments.

49

It is useful to set out some of the circumstances which could inhibit mining investment in those countries and a loss of production capacity. Also to be considered is the worst-case circumstances under which changing political allegiances could lead the governments of one or more of these countries to deny their mineral exports to their neighbors and allies of the West. This possibility must be considered within the context of the political world that could evolve over the next decade or so.

It is perhaps this political denial of natural resource exports from Mexico that is the most serious. For internal and external reasons, Mexico could well have a Communist government within a decade. Mexico's difficulties are both domestic and external. Domestically, the economy is slowing down while its current account balance of payments is widening and its gross foreign borrowing requirements approach $20 billion.

These trends will deepen the fissures in the economy, the most serious of which continues to be the growing disparity between the rich and the poor.

Due to increased oil production, there is new wealth creation in the country, but no new wealth distribution. The government has failed in its program of land distribution (EJIDOS). There are an estimated four million landless peasants who have petitioned for land and are waiting for word from the government. The truth is that the government does not have any more land to give, yet it continues to accept petitions. Landless laborers exert pressure on the system through invasion, rural guerrilla activities and petitions to the government.

The government has concentrated on improving education and medical facilities, with some success. Unfortunately, economic rewards have not been forthcoming; the peasants still have little hope of ever leaving their misery behind.

Membership in a labor union is no longer a path to more income. Mexico has institutionalized its labor movement. The leaders are not representative of rank and file members and are often just as corrupt as government leaders. Union members often find their strikes achieve nothing when their leaders settle the dispute without gaining worker demands. Because per capita income is higher in the city than in rural areas, the cities have been flooded with unskilled labor willing to work for low wages. Companies depend on these new rural workers who have just arrived. Union insurgency tends to arise from among the more skilled, better-paid workers in the more modern sectors of the economy. These workers are young and better educated. As they become politicized their dissent will increase.

An estimated 50 percent of the population is under 15 years old. Most of these people are undernourished. Mexico City has an estimated population of 12 to 13 million people. The government does seem aware of Mexico City's major draw on the rural population and is trying to encourage portions of its population to settle elsewhere. Pemex, the state-owned oil monopoly, is in Villahermosa near the new oil fields, and other industries are being encouraged to move into other districts in hopes of generating jobs and income in other regions. As more and more people reach working age, the competition for already scarce jobs will increase. One-half of the working-age population is either underemployed or unemployed.

The bracero program, which allowed Mexican workers to work in the United States, ended in 1964 at the insistence of the American unions. Since then, one million Mexicans have been caught crossing the border illegally. The number of Mexicans who cross safely is probably double that. Should the U.S. attempt to cut off this escape route, there could be an explosion in Mexico.

Equally fundamental to Mexico's difficulties is the Indian population of 30 million, of which the Mayans are the second largest representatives. They live in depressed conditions in southeastern Mexico and spill over into Guatemala, Honduras, El Salvador and Belize. The Mayans have long endured the hardships of peonage on the latifundia estates. When they began resisting the encroachment of the oil development on their traditional life, they were set upon by latifundistas, police and the Mexican army. Working 16 hours a day for a wage of about one dollar, and seeing themselves displaced by the oil boom, Indians nursed a resentment that escalated to hatred and violence. Mayans in Guatemala have vowed to assist their ethnic brothers in Mexico after installing a revolutionary government in their country.

The format of revolution that carried the Sandinistas to victory in Nicaragua is being developed in Guatemala with the Indian component added. The Indians are counting on, and accepting, Marxist organizations as well as sympathetic church sources. Weapons smuggled into Guatemala are being provided to the Indian insurgents. As the war escalates Indians who are pushed northward eventually take refuge in Mexico. There, news concerning the Mayan revolt in Guatemala soon spreads to Mexican Mayans.

The Mexican government has sought to correct the image of its police and military as protectors of the landowners and oppressors of the impoverished and displaced Indians. But the economic lot of the Indian has worsened steadily since the petroleum boom. Income disparity, always a serious social problem in Mexico, has widened perceptibly in the southeastern oil-producing areas. That is where Mexico meets Guatemala, where Indian alienation is growing.

It is at this stage that the external difficulties start to impinge on the internal problems. A contagion of unrest runs through Central America.

The center for this offensive is Nicaragua, where roads have been constructed for heavy equipment, and airfields extended to take large transport planes. Regular shipments of military equipment are allegedly being made from Cuba and by sea from North Korea. In addition, there are suggestions of a PLO connection with the insurgents. Fresh arms and equipment may be going from Nicaragua to El Salvador, Guatemala and Honduras, and Costa Rica now feels the pressure.

Thus, there must be a real risk that within a decade Mexico, which is already moving toward a nationalistic/socialistic orientation, will have a Communist government. It is worth mentioning that since 1968 Moscow has regarded its embassy in Mexico as one of its four or five most important embassies anywhere in the world, and today has one of its largest KGB staff working out of it.

While these political developments are unlikely to prevent Mexico from developing the country's rich mineral resources, they will inhibit foreign-company participation. Equally important, exports may be denied access to the U.S. Certainly they cannot be counted on to continue over the next 15 years.

The comments that follow on Australia and Canada must by definition be more subjective because both countries are members of the OECD and because both are more mature economically and politically than Mexico. There are two principal aspects that will help fashion policy toward the mining industry. First there is the general direction of political trends—will the next move be more to the left or to the right? And second, there will be the manner in which policy is directed toward the mining industry itself.

The internal political direction of both countries will be influenced by the general trend of world politics. Two decades of creeping socialism and financial irresponsibility have brought the Western world to a crossroads in post–World War II history. The road to the left will lead to embracing the interventionist policies of a state-controlled nation, whereas the turn to the right means accepting the disciplines of a free-market society.

The turn to the left is clearly a "soft" option, and the turn to the right is obviously a long and bumpy road. There have been some tentative signs suggesting that electorates are moving cautiously toward the latter, but it is too soon to know whether this presages a permanent trend or is a simple political reaction to previous weak governments.

Examples of this are the U.K. and the U.S. There was an initial desire for change reflected in the election of advocates of more conservative policies, but in pursuing these policies these conservative governments inflicted a good deal of pain. A restlessness among the electorate suggests that the move to the right that has been seen in the last two years will not continue for long. In effect, the choice before democratic governments over the next five years will continue to be either high unemployment or high inflation.

Simultaneously, the attempts by the Soviet Union to divide the Western Alliance, and in the process make NATO impotent, should not be ignored because, if successful, it would suggest that there will be a widespread move to the left in Western Europe.

These comments are made because in Canada, in particular, the political trends seem fairly well established toward socialism and nationalism, as has been made apparent in recent energy and mining policies. For overseas companies, the investment screening process is far more formal and considerably more stringent and discriminating than in other developed countries. New foreign investment is subject to review by the Foreign Investment Review Authority (FIRA), which operates in relative secrecy and has exercised expanded discretionary authority.

In addition to making it difficult for established foreign-controlled firms to expand in Canada, discriminatory policies actually aim at the disinvestment of such firms. This is particularly true in the energy industry under the proposed national energy policy (NEP), and these changes may be the precursor of a new mining policy. In effect, by placing foreign-controlled or -owned energy companies at a severe disadvantage through taxation, leasing rights and ownership restrictions, discriminatory exploration and development incentives, etc., the government has eroded the market value of the Canadian assets of some foreign companies. Then the government encouraged

Canadian firms to acquire those assets—for example, Conoco's dis-investment of Hudson Bay Oil and Gas, Amoco's sale of Cyprus An-viln and the Canadian Development Corp.'s purchase of Texas Gulf's Kidd Creek operations. Indeed, in the February–July 1981 period, government and private interests in Canada spent over $5 billion in "Canadianization" transactions that might not otherwise have occurred.

These developments, however, continue a trend that has been developing for some ten years. Despite these difficulties, overseas money has continued to flow into the country to develop the coun-try's mineral resources. The attractions are obvious: a legal and tax system that is compatible with most other developed countries', a country richly endowed in mineral resources, an established in-frastructure, an educated labor force and the knowledge that should nationalization take place (for example, Kidd Creek), the terms of-fered would be reasonably fair.

It is perhaps stating the obvious that during the next two decades more nationalization of the mining industry will take place. Overseas investment will continue to move into Canada because of its attrac-tive conditions, relative to other areas. No matter what type of gov-ernment is in office, mineral exports to the U.S.—or to the Western world—will not be denied, since they are an important contributor to foreign exchange. Nonetheless, there will be periods of tension and lower investment in the mining industry. It remains to be seen, therefore, whether Canada can fulfill its mining potential.

Many of the comments made about Canada are equally relevant to Australia. Australia, however, is unlikely to follow the national-ization route. Recently, foreign-owned companies have noted an improvement in the investment environment. Authorization for in-vestment is given by the Foreign Investment Review Board and is linked to a number of preconditions or "offsets" aimed at promoting greater participation of Australian capital.

The political system, however, can cause quite dramatic changes in policy, as elections are held every three years, and there is a wide disparity in policy formulation between the two parties. The ruling Liberal Country party coalition, which was returned to office in Oc-tober 1980 with a reduced majority, has provided a more farsighted and attractive investment environment for both overseas-controlled and domestic mining companies. Given the nature of Australian pol-itics, it is questionable whether the Liberal Country party can con-tinue to be elected.

A second impediment to investment in the mining sector is labor. Australian unions seem to have inherited many of the worst features of their English compatriots—truculence, low productivity, strikes and high wage demands. A third impediment is unfavorable capital and operating costs relative to some other mining areas of the world, due to the high degree of infrastructure required to be built and the high level of labor costs. A fourth drawback is environmental issues and environmental planning. The last point varies between the states, with such planning being particularly stringent in New South Wales. Environmental issues have become social problems, as the aluminum industry discovered over its proposed smelter sites in the Hunter Valley district of New South Wales, and as Alcoa found out when hearings were held for the construction of the Portland smelter. In addition, the aborigines now seem to discover local tribal sites on most major mine developments and metallurgical plant construction sites.

While none of these factors will preclude local or foreign investment, combined they will prevent Australia from fulfilling its mineral potential. The recent cancellation of a number of aluminum smelter projects could be attributed partly to depressed demand and prices, but also to the fact that capital and operating costs became unfavorable by comparison with those in the United States.

In summary, then, the lines seem to be drawn for countries surrounding Mexico, and Mexico itself, to become Marxist-oriented states over the next decade, with probable effects on the direction of natural resources exports. Although politics in Australia and Canada could prevent both countries from fulfilling their mineral potential, their exports will continue to be available to the West.

5

Third World Rallying Cry: A New International Economic Order

The U.S., Western Europe and Japan have long looked to the Third World[1] for important supplies of critical and strategic minerals, most notably cobalt, tin, bauxite and copper, but including a wide range of other minerals as well. Much of this Third World production came from mines developed, financed and owned by large transnational companies based in the industrial nations. Typically, the ores were shipped in raw or semiprocessed form, manufactured into finished products in the industrial countries and there consumed, or returned to the Third World as finished goods.

This trade carried certain benefits to both the owners of the mining companies and to the Third World host countries. It assured a supply of essential raw materials to the industrial nations, and the mines provided jobs, government revenues and resources for the development of the mineral-producing countries. But in recent years the developing world has asserted with growing determination its demands for far greater control of its natural resources and a bigger share of the total revenue generated. This Third World campaign for economic reform has come to be known as the New International Economic Order, or NIEO. Only a small part of the program has actually been implemented, but the philosophy of the NIEO has profoundly affected the thinking and the political behavior of many of the Third World countries. The NIEO could vastly change the trade relationships that have long existed between the developed and the developing countries and, in a worst-case scenario, could lead to a denial of raw materials to the industrial world.

The concept of the NIEO arose largely from a bloc of developing countries that called themselves the Group of 77. Membership in the bloc, which is loose and informal, is now over 120. It includes many of the world's economic basket cases, the poorest of the poor, as well as some of the relatively well-developed nations in the middle, such as Mexico, Brazil and Venezuela. The Group of 77 also includes some members such as India, with strategic and political importance to the West far beyond their role as suppliers of raw materials. China is not a member of the Group of 77, although it considers itself a "developing" country.

Rita Hauser, a former U.S. representative to the U.N. Commission on Human Rights, has described the West's reaction to the proclamation of the New International Economic Order:

> That document, when it was launched, was greeted by the West with laughs and incredulity, because it was a hodgepodge of concepts, many poorly thought out, most of which ran counter to our most deeply held views. It stressed the right of resource countries to expropriate freely, to take property which had theretofore been granted to the companies of other countries under solemnly negotiated treaties, sometimes without much compensation. It reflected a moment in history when Third World countries were asserting their right as they saw it over the resources that were located in their countries. They were, in effect, trying to reverse decades of colonialism. The moral and political argument that they made was . . . that during the colonial period they had been raped of their assets, their resources and their people. They had been deprived and they were in the abominably poor position they were in because of that history. One could spend a great deal of time negating that position, but that is the underlying political position that they held.
>
> Speeches at the U.N. consist of attacks on the colonial world, in which we are lumped though we were not much of a colonial power, and they asserted their right to get back at the developed world by withholding resources and the renegotiation of all forms of concessions.
>
> The NIEO is not new, not international (each acts in his own interest with little concern about the world's interest); it is not economic but fundamentally political in that it represents the politics of wanting a greater share of their own resources and of the resources which we are coming to call the common heritage of mankind, including the Antarctic and the moon. The U.S. and the developed world will spend most of the resources getting there, but the rest of the world wants to share in the return.
>
> We have a serious problem, and have to confront it. . . . The Third World makes up the majority by far of the members of the U.N., and through the means of renegotiation of basic concessions, they are asserting a fair stranglehold over the developed world for

these fundamental resources. At the same time, because it is political, they refuse to deal with the most important event that has
happened in the last decade, that has really impoverished most of
these countries. That is the enormous increase in the price of oil
which they have to pay and cannot pay. The Gulf countries give
them a pittance in terms of assistance in development. But the fact
is they are being broken and busted by the ever-increasing oil
bill. . . . Yet when a debate comes up in the U.N. in terms of what
is happening at OPEC and the enormous increase in oil prices,
you will not find a single one of those nations lining up to argue
against OPEC with the West, because fundamentally they con-
ceive of themselves politically as anti-West, anti-colonial, allied
politically and morally with the Third World even if it will kill
them in the process.[2]

NIEO has implications far beyond its immediate effect on the
price and availability of raw materials. It is an effort to redesign
the world economy to favor developing nations. It is part of the
Third World's broader rejection of many of the Western-created institutions that have governed international trade, aid and currency
relationships since 1944. That was the year in which the not-yet-
victorious Allied powers met at Bretton Woods, New Hampshire, to
create a system of monetary controls, fixed exchange rates and international assistance to function in the postwar world. The Allies
hoped to prevent a recurrence of the economic crises and chronic
instability that had helped to lead to World War II.

Out of Bretton Woods came two institutions that despite failures,
criticism and changing political currents are still functioning nearly
four decades later. The International Monetary Fund was created to
promote international monetary cooperation and promote stability in
foreign exchange rates by making each nation responsible for maintaining the strength of its own currency. The International Bank for
Reconstruction and Development, better known as the World Bank,
was designed originally to smooth the transition from a wartime to a
peacetime economy and to aid war-damaged nations; it has evolved
largely into an international agency for economic development, with
funds largely contributed by the industrial nations.

Implicit in the Bretton Woods agreements were assumptions that
currency exchange rates and the price of gold would remain relatively stable, that monetary stability and a rising pattern of investment would be the key to national development and that all

countries not in the Communist bloc would follow the Western pattern for economic development. This was, quite simply, a Western-designed system intended to deal with a world seen through Western eyes. For nearly three decades it worked reasonably well. With the price of gold fixed by the U.S. Treasury and the dollar serving as the world's basic reserve currency, a high degree of currency stability was achieved. Europe and Japan staged an astonishing recovery from the havoc of World War II. Investment and production led the way to a rising standard of living in most of the countries that had signed the original Bretton Woods agreement, and in Germany and Japan, which joined the system later.

But elsewhere in the world, prosperity was far more elusive. In the 30 years that followed 1944, more than 75 new countries emerged from the colonial system to achieve political independence. Almost all joined the U.N., the IMF and the World Bank. But these new nations were significantly different from those that had created the Bretton Woods system. Many of their economies were heavily dependent upon one or two basic products, mineral or agricultural. This left their economies highly vulnerable to crop failures, price recessions and changing market demands. Often the means of production, plantations or mines, were controlled by foreign owners. Many of the new nations lacked the basic infrastructures needed for economic growth—roads, railroads, communications—and they lacked the resources to provide the basic services of education, health care and social welfare. Illiteracy was high, disease prevalent and poverty pervasive.

Bad economic conditions were aggravated by political instability, by lack of sound administrative structures and in some cases by pervasive corruption and by the tendency of new rulers to borrow money for grandiose developments that brought little benefit to the mass of the people. Presidential palaces, great stadiums and national airlines became the new international status symbols.

In 1974 the U.N. General Assembly met in special session to discuss the issue of raw materials and development. Inflation triggered by OPEC oil price increases was causing economic havoc. During the special session, the Third World countries presented a more united front than ever before with their demands for fundamental changes in the world's economic ground rules, first to slow the widening of the gap between the rich and poor nations, and second, to start to close it. Out of this debate came the Declaration and the

Program of Action on the Establishment of a New International Economic Order. These documents clearly reflected an emerging political viewpoint of former colonies that had become sovereign states without gaining economic power.

The Declaration got right to cases with the assertion that "the greatest and most significant achievement during the last decades has been the independence from colonial and alien domination of a large number of peoples and nations." Yet, it noted, "The benefits of technological progress are not shared equitably by all members of the international community. The developing countries which constitute 70 percent of the world's population account for only 30 percent of the world's income."

As a step toward evening the imbalance of economic strength, the Declaration called for "full permanent sovereignty of every state over its natural resources and all economic activities . . . including the right to naturalization or transfer of ownership to its nationals." On the question of compensation for nationalized properties, the Declaration was silent.

The argument of the Third World countries can be summarized in a few key points:

On the roots of Third World poverty: "The entire industrial production of developing countries is less than that of the Federal Republic of Germany," says a United Nations document.[3] This condition is attributed to the slow development of the Third World countries during the colonial period: "Although roads and railroads and some of the other basic amenities necessary to rule and exploit the economic resources of the colonies were built by colonial rulers, they actively discouraged industrial development. The colonies were confined to producing cheap raw materials for factories in the ruling countries and buying manufactured goods in return." In the postcolonial period, according to this view, the world monetary system founded at Bretton Woods was stacked against producers of raw materials to the benefit of the industrial nations. "The world is still in search of a monetary system with more stability than the current one and less rigidity than that of Bretton Woods," says this document.

On hunger in the Third World: Although world food production is adequate to sustain all the people on the globe, poor distribution leaves 400 million people undernourished and perhaps two to three times that number suffering from varying degrees of malnutrition.

To feed their people, the developing countries import $20 billion of food grains each year, mostly from developed countries. Third World food production is increasing but not rapidly enough. Storage and transportaion facilities are inadequate. Direct foreign aid from developed countries is only a partial solution; assistance with technology, scientific research and fertilizers is urgently needed; so are new pricing techniques and a restructuring of the world economy.

On the Third World's debt burden: Total debts owed by the Third World are so great—an estimated $400 billion in 1981—that debt service absorbs up to half of all foreign earnings in some countries, limiting their ability to buy the food and technology they need to improve production. Rising costs of manufactured imports and falling prices for raw materials have aggravated the problem. Some rescheduling of debt may be necessary to avoid default.

On raw materials: For the developing world as a whole, sales of raw materials account for 85 percent of foreign income (63 percent if oil is excluded). To mitigate the effect of excessive fluctuation in raw material prices, some mechanism for the stabilization of prices is essential.

Acting through the U.N., the Third World nations have advanced a series of far-reaching proposals for reform aimed at alleviating their very real economic problems. Presented as resolutions in the U.N. General Assembly or through U.N. conferences and agencies and often adopted by "consensus" (in other words, without a vote), the proposals may be seen as political demands upon the developed nations, which are being asked to pay the bills. An example was Resolution 3362, adopted by the General Assembly in 1975. It demanded:

• Transfer of technology and scientific resources to Third World countries.

• Concerted efforts to help developing countries expand productivity, trade, export earnings.

• Expanded borrowing power for the developing countries in the IMF, and a greater voice by the Third World in the agency's decisions.

• Expansion of food production in the developing countries through increased aid for agricultural production; action to build and maintain world grain reserves.

More specific programs have emerged in later conferences and documents. The common goal is to narrow the wide economic gap that now separates the developed and developing nations. The latter call for transfer of wealth in the form of grants, aid, scientific technology and means of production from the wealthier to the poor. The goals are frequently clearer than the means to accomplish them.

The U.S., Western Europe and Japan frequently cite reservations about the scope or effectiveness of specific proposals, but have usually agreed with the overall aims of the proposals as guidelines.

The developing countries have called upon the developed world to contribute one percent of their gross national product to the Third World in the form of direct government aid and other forms of assistance. They want these aid programs channeled through agencies to be controlled by the recipient nations rather than by the donors, as in the past.

The West's reaction has been guarded. France's socialist president François Mitterand has indicated sympathy with the proposals but without committing his country to greatly expanded contributions. In the U.S., the reaction has been even more cautious. At the United Nations, American spokesmen urge the developing nations to give market forces a free rein to function, liberating "the energies of their own citizens working in their own interest," as one U.S. spokesman put it.

This closely reflects the view of President Ronald Reagan, who reminded an audience in 1981 that in the previous two years, non-OPEC developing countries' exports to the U.S. earned more than the entire developing world has received from the World Bank in the last 36 years. The president has called for negotiations between developed and developing nations to promote trade liberalization, development of resources and food production and improvement of the investment climate. His message was received with a notable lack of enthusiasm among Third World representatives.

The Administration has indicated that it will continue to support such international lending institutions as the IMF and the World Bank, though it has not specified the scope of this support. Presumably that is subject to negotiation.

As a means of stabilizing prices of the Third World's raw materials, the United Nations Conference on Trade and Development proposed the negotiation of a price stabilization plan to be known as the Integrated Program for Commodities. Proposed at first to cover 18 mine, farm and forest products, the list of commodities was later expanded to 22. The plan envisages creation of a central fund of about $6 billion to stabilize the prices of individual commodities through the use of floor prices, ceiling prices and trigger prices that would activate buying or selling programs. As Bhaskar P. Menon, an official of the U.N.'s Division for Economic and Social Information, explained: "This would be an attempt to insert a kind of cushion between the producers and the consuming markets, so the shocks of the business cycle in the consuming countries would not be directly transmitted to the poverty-stricken countries." The minerals tentatively included in the program are bauxite, copper, iron ore, manganese, tin and phosphates, but the outlook for completion of a far-ranging price stabilization program is far from clear.

The Group of 77's demands have been received warily in the developed countries, where the demands are regarded as large and unrealistic, but by sheer numbers and political power the Group holds bargaining power. The struggle will continue. Numbering a large majority of all U.N. members as well as the huge nations of China and India, the developing nations carry a political impact heightened by the certain realization that the industrial nations cannot look forward to a life of peace and prosperity in a world inhabited by a huge majority of impoverished, deprived and restless billions.

It is also true that the economic prosperity of the developed countries depends in great degree on markets in the developing nations. They are customers for exports of consumer products, services and capital. More than one-third of all U.S. exports each year go to developing nations. Sales to the Third World are even higher for Japan, a little lower for Western Europe.

By the vagaries of the economic cycle, the period since the NEIO emerged as a political cause has been a time of recession in many mineral industries. Mines started in the 1960s and the early '70s were brought to completion, industrial demand was relatively soft, and except for chrome during the Zimbabwe revolution and cobalt because of the 1978 invasion of Zaire, most minerals have been in relatively good supply. How long this will continue is a matter of great concern to industrialists and military planners of the West.

Nationalizations of mining properties in Chile, Cuba, Zaire and Zambia in the 1960s and 1970s brought home to Western investors that a new risk factor had to be taken into account in planning new investments—the risk of seizure by host governments. Partly as a result of this concern, mining investment in the Third World slowed almost to a standstill in the 1970s. The mines that were not built were the mines that would have come on stream in the late 1970s and the decade of the 1980s. Their absence may be felt in the years ahead.

Mining investment has continued, but principally in the developed nations of the U.S., Canada and Australia, where political risk is minimal. The pattern is shown by these statistics from the U.S. Department of Commerce, showing total U.S. investments in mining and smelting in place at the end of each year during the 1970s:[4]

Year	Developed Countries (in millions of dollars)	Developing Countries
1970	$3,286	$2,119
1971	3,569	2,218
1972	3,400	2,267
1973	3,773	2,265
1974	4,007	1,784
1975	4,398	2,150
1976	4,750	2,309
1977	4,152	1,846
1978	4,034	1,699
1979	4,195	1,746
1980	4,487	2,006

What becomes clear is that while American mining companies modestly increased their investments in the developed countries during the last decade, investment in the Third World remained essentially static or on a declining curve if the effect of inflation is taken into account.

This pattern of diminishing investment in the Third World seems likely to continue as long as wholesale nationalization remains a threat. Charles Barber, chairman of the multinational mining company Asarco, said in a speech in 1980:

> You must have an element of certainty as to fiscal policy, tax policy, access policy. For about ten years now there has been almost a total lack of new commitments to additional [mining] capacity. This has been concealed because projects conceived and committed in the 1960s have been coming into production through the middle '70s. . . . But because of the ten-year lag and the long lead

time involved, we are now built into scarcities of some of these essential materials including copper, lead and zinc, from which there is no escape even if the world changes tomorrow.[5]

While Third World spokesmen frequently call for increased foreign investment in their countries as a key to lifting the standard of living for their people, their politicians in many cases make it difficult for Western companies to risk long-term investment in assets that cannot be recovered. It is a conflict that the Third World leaders will have to resolve.

Simon Strauss, a former vice-chairman of Asarco, estimates that at least 15 large and commercially viable deposits of copper and related ores have been identified, explored and subjected to preliminary engineering work in Third World countries. Yet, says this executive, "Not one project has gotten off the boards since the middle of 1974 until this year [1981]." The 1981 project was in Papua New Guinea, where a consortium of Australian, American and German companies, assured by the Papua New Guinea government that their investment will not be nationalized, has begun work on a large copper mine. The companies were also encouraged by the presence of a substantial gold deposit in the overburden above the copper ore; this will provide an early return on investment in a very long-term project.

Elsewhere in the Third World, such projects are unlikely to be duplicated until a combination of higher metal prices and a secure political climate makes such investments as attractive as, say, U.S. government securities, paying a safe high return. What this means to consumers of metals is that production from existing mines in the Third World will gradually decline as ore bodies are exhausted.

A publication on the NEIO called *Global Dialogue*[6] perhaps unintentionally illustrates the attitude of Western mining executives. The cover design of the pamphlet shows five Western faces presumably listening to Third World speakers. The only happy face among them belongs to one man who has removed his earphones and is no longer listening.

6

The Resource War: It Is Real

In any analysis of the world outlook in critical and strategic materials, the role of the Soviet Union assumes crucial importance. Historically, the USSR has sold minerals to the West to pay for its imports of Western technology and grain. Soviet exports include some of the most critical of metals, notably manganese, chromium, the platinum group and titanium. At one time or another the Soviets have halted or severely reduced their sales of all of these materials and others to their Western customers.

Some of these cutbacks were the result of accidents in Soviet mines, others were attributed to the sheer inefficiency of the state-controlled mining industry, and others to the growing appetite of the Soviets' own civilian and defense industries. A cutoff of Soviet chromite sales in 1950 was almost surely related to Soviet planning for what became the Korean War.

Beyond the Soviet Union's role as a primary producer of minerals is its position as a center of political influence in the Third World. As this influence grows in the mineral-rich region of Southern Africa, it opens the possibility that the Soviets through control of natural resources in their own country and their influence in the Third World could apply a damaging strategy of resource denial against the West. A growing number of analysts feel that this strategy has advanced from theory to threat; they are calling it the Soviet Union's Resource War Against the West. This is a subtle form of aggression, insidious in its effect, potentially damaging in peacetime and morally threatening in war, yet almost beneath the threshold of rational response. The West must develop a countervailing strategy.

Sovietologists have delved into the literature of Soviet thought to find the roots of the Resource War. As early as 1921, Josef Stalin wrote:

> If Europe and America may be called the front or the arena of the major battles between socialism and imperialism, the unequal na-

tions and the colonies, with their raw materials, fuel, food and vast store of manpower, must be regarded as the rear, the reserve of imperialism. To win a war it is necessary not to triumph at the front, but also to revolutionize the enemy's rear, his reserves.[1]

Another Soviet leader, Nikita Khrushchev, made a similar point at the University of Jakarta in 1960:

Afro-Asian countries play an essential part in limiting aggression in an economic respect. They are important suppliers of raw materials for the Western powers. The supporters of aggression understand that when the majority of Afro-Asian countries follow a peace-loving policy, they are unable to count on the use of the rich resources of Afro-Asian countries in their aggressive plans.[2]

Rear Admiral William C. Mott, who testified July 8, 1981, in a Congressional inquiry into the Resource War, told the House subcommittee on Africa that he had personally interviewed a Soviet KGB defector then in British protective custody and was told, "the Soviet government has been paying much attention to the 'resource war' since the mid-forties." The defector, Ilya Dzhirkvelov, volunteered to Admiral Mott that the KGB had been gathering intelligence worldwide on the availability of resources with the purpose of finding ways to inflict damage upon the Western economies. "Stalin's goal of depriving the West of the mineral resources of the planet is still pursued," he told his interrogator.

Some highly placed American officials have also become convinced that the Resource War is real and threatening, if undeclared. General Alexander Haig, before his appointment as secretary of state, told the House subcommittee on Mines and Mining on September 18, 1980:

As one assesses the recent step up of Soviet proxy activity in the Third World—in Angola, Ethiopia, Southern Yemen, Northern Yemen, Southeast Asia, Central America and the Caribbean, and the . . . unprecedented invasion of Afghanistan by regular Soviet forces—then one can only conclude that the era of the "resource war" has arrived.

William Casey, director of the CIA, in a speech before the United States Chamber of Commerce, voiced concern at the growing Soviet influence in the Third World and its increasing ability to project military power into the resource-rich regions vital to the West.

The vulnerability of Western and Japanese mineral supply lines was pointed up by yet another expert. Rear Admiral Robert J. Hanks, now retired, speaking as a representative of the Institute for Foreign Policy Analysis, told the House Mines and Mining subcommittee on September 18, 1980:

> It has been said that there are two great "treasure houses" in our modern industrial world. The first is in the Persian Gulf where the bulk of the globe's petroleum energy is to be found and without which Western economies could not survive. The other lies in Southern Africa. Here, the indispensable commodities are minerals and metals equally essential to the modern industrial process. Complete stoppage or even a significant reduction in the flow of these "treasure house" materials to the United States, the nations of Western Europe, and to Japan could generate economic and therefore political catastrophe.

Not all observers are convinced that the Soviet Union's strategy truly constitutes a Resource War, or that pro-Soviet regimes could successfully deny to the West the export commodities on which their economies depend for foreign exchange. An essential argument of this viewpoint is that the economic needs of the developing countries will force them to market their products in the West whatever their ideology or their relations with the Soviet Union.

This view seems to disregard the example of Iran, where a radical anti-Western (though non-Communist) regime cut off virtually all of the nation's oil exports to the West. This occurred in part as a voluntary act of denial by the regime, a form of self-immolation, but it also resulted from sheer confusion and economic disruption attendant to the Iranian revolution and later the war with Iraq. A nation in violent political transition can hardly be a reliable producer of minerals, whatever its economic needs or political motives. This is true in the case of oil and probably even more true in the case of underground mines, whose power supplies, pumps and mining machinery are highly vulnerable to acts of sabotage.

In June, 1980, the Pittsburgh World Affairs Council convened a conference of experts on mineral supply and national policy, and later published a study entitled *The Resource War in 3-D—Depen-*

dency, Diplomacy, Defense.[3] Among the conclusions reached by the experts at the conference:

• U.S. dependence on strategic minerals threatens the nation's economic well-being and national security.

• In the competition for oil and nonfuel minerals, "the Soviet Union must be regarded as a hostile state, whose leaders may be attempting to injure the U.S. and its allies by impeding their access to strategic minerals."

• The U.S. should reorient its defense and foreign policies to take this reality into account and, in concert with its allies, act to ensure the security of mineral sources and supply lines for the Free World.

In a paper presented at the Pittsburgh conference and in other speeches and publications, Daniel I. Fine of the Mining and Mineral Resource Institute of Massachusetts Institute of Technology has developed a thesis that challenges the older view of the Soviet Union as a producer and provider to the West of a long shopping list of strategic minerals. Fine believes that the Soviet Union is nearing the end of its role as a significant exporter of iron ore, manganese, vanadium, titanium and lithium; that its production and export of chromite ore is diminishing; and that its exports of platinum metals are undependable because of production difficulties and the growing demand of the USSR's own chemical industries. In addition, says Fine, the Soviet Union's dependence on imports is growing in such strategic metals and ores as molybdenum, bauxite, cobalt, tungsten, antimony, fluorspar, tin, nickel and lead. Thus it will become a competitor in world markets for these materials, with important implications for supply patterns and price movements in the future.

The Soviet Union has demonstrated its readiness to make forays into metal markets for political rather than commercial motives. In this context, raw materials may be seen as another weapon in the Soviet arsenal in its long-term struggle for power and prestige. Fine reports that in 1981 Soviet representatives offered to sell 4,000 tons of nickel in North America at $2.57 a pound, at a time when the world price was $2.87 a pound. This may have been an attempt to inflict commercial damage on two Canadian-based producers of nickel, INCO and Falconbridge, both of which were suffering at the time from weak markets and poor sales. If either firm could be weakened or driven out of nickel production, the West would become dependent upon the Soviet bloc for supplies of this highly strategic metal. Fine saw the Soviet maneuver as an effort to open a market in North America for nickel from Cuban mines. After expropriating the mines from their American owners more than two decades ago, the Cubans finally seem to be getting them into effective production.

In Fine's analysis, the Soviet Union has also pursued its outreach strategy in the markets for tantalum and titanium. The USSR was long assumed to be self-sufficient in tantalum, a relatively scarce metal essential in electronics and therefore in military applications. In 1980 the Soviet Union began buying tantalum abroad at a rate that suggested either production difficulties or stockpiling or both. The Soviets are reported to have assigned a team of geologists and mining experts to try to restore production in old Portuguese mines in Mozambique.

In the case of titanium, the pattern of diminishing Soviet production and a determined outreach to foreign sources was even clearer. For many years the Soviet Union was a major supplier of titanium to the U.S., Japan and Western Europe. This strong, lightweight metal is used in missiles, high-performance aircraft and submarines. In 1979 the Soviets increased their prices for titanium; then they began cutting back on foreign sales, first to the United States, then to Japan, France and West Germany. The notification to Germany was made, as it happened, within 72 hours of Bonn's announcement that it would consider deploying Pershing missiles on its soil, a move strongly opposed by the Soviet Union. During 1979 the Soviets also sent a purchasing mission to Australia to try to sew up a long-term purchasing agreement in rutile, the ore from which titanium sponge is produced.

The motive behind these moves suddenly became clear on January 1, 1980 as the Soviets launched their invasion of Afghanistan. Their metal market maneuvers of 1979 had clearly been part of a preinvasion stockpiling and conservation scheme to shore up their military preparations. In the wake of the Afghanistan invasion, Australia cut off a planned Soviet purchase of 2,000 metric tons of rutile, about 7 percent of Moscow's apparent needs, thus contributing a moderate counteraction in a Resource War that can work both ways.

Daniel Fine has concluded that the Soviet Union is engaged in a massive change of policy, from a strategy of self-reliance in mineral supply to an outward strategy calling for increasing access to world resources. While the Soviet Union comes closer to mineral self-sufficiency than any other major economy, it is still import-dependent for a significant number of minerals. Beyond that, its leaders may have decided to reach out to foreign suppliers, saving their own huge mineral reserves in the difficult and inaccessible Siberian Arctic for future exploitation—safe in the deep freeze, so to speak. Presumably when the world's more accessible mineral resources are exhausted, the Soviets will be able to extract an even higher price and greater political leverage from those frozen assets.

The Soviet Union's policy of reaching out to world resources has also affected the Eastern Bloc nations, which since the 1950s had profited from the "Bucharest principle," under which the Soviet Union sold raw materials to its COMECON partners at less than world prices. Now the Eastern Bloc nations also must enter the world markets to supply their mineral requirements.

This shift in Soviet resource strategy may help to explain other Soviet foreign policy initiatives, including a massive preoccupation with Southern Africa. Since the mid-1970s, the Soviets have shipped $4.5 billion in weapons to Africa, most of it into Central and Southern Africa. They sold $85 million of MIG jet fighters and other weapons to Zambia, which was in far greater need of internal development and food production. With the help of Soviet arms, Marxist regimes took control of Angola and Mozambique.

In Angola, a Soviet-armed Cuban force of 20,000 serves as a mercenary army protecting the government from the anti-Marxist Jonas Savimbi and his UNITA forces in the Angolan countryside. The Cubans almost surely had a hand in training the guerrillas who raided the cobalt mines in Zaire's Shaba province in 1978, and the Cubans, along with Russian and East European advisors, are trying to whip Sam Nujoma's South West Africa Peoples Organization into a fighting force capable of dislodging the South Africans from Namibia by force if not by vote. The SWAPO bases in Angola are not just guerrilla camps in the jungle; they include radar and air defense bases (or did until a South African force destroyed them in 1981), with SAM-3 and SAM-6 antiaircraft missiles and a contingent of Soviet and East German advisors and commanders.

It is easy to see in this Soviet buildup a long-range strategy aimed not just at installing friendly regimes in the former colonies but at building up a conventional force capable of threatening South Africa itself, the region's greatest treasure-house of minerals, and controlling the seaborne traffic around the Cape of Good Hope. In this strategy, the Cuban mercenaries serve as a mobile force, not just guarding the government in Angola, but capable of mounting a serious military threat against neighboring states not yet fallen under Communist control. If while building up friendly regimes and threatening unfriendly ones, this strategy also succeeds in weaking its Western adversaries and denying them resources, so much the better from the Moscow perspective. Controlling both their own resources in strategic metals and those in Southern Africa, they would own a near monopoly on supplies of some vital materials (see chart).

SOUTHERN AFRICAN and USSR PERCENTAGES of WORLD'S RESERVES of SELECTED MINERAL COMMODITIES

Commodity	Southern Africa's Percentage of World's Reserves	USSR's Percentage of World's Reserves	Combined Southern Africa and USSR Percentage
1. Platinum Group Metals	86	13	99
2. Manganese Ore	53	45	98
3. Vanadium	64	33	97
4. Chrome Ore	95	1	96
5. Diamonds	83	4	87
6. Gold	50	19	69
7. Vermiculite	60	N.A.	60
8. Fluorspar	46	4	50
9. Asbestos	25	25	50
10. Iron Ore	5	42	47
11. Uranium	27	13	40
12. Columbium-Tantalite	38	N.A.	38
13. Cobalt	25	N.A.	25
14. Copper	13	9	22
15. Titanium	5	16	21
16. Nickel	12	7	19
17. Zinc	10	8	18
18. Lead	4	13	17
19. Coal	5	10	15
20. Phosphate Rock	8	4	12
21. Tin	4	6	10
22. Antimony	4	5	9

Source: E. F. Andrews, Vice-President for Materials and Services, Allegheny Ludlum Industries Inc., June 1979

The evolution of Southern Africa in the 1970s into a cockpit of nationalist ambitions, guerrilla movements with international connections, and direct big-power rivalries is an instructive example of the development of the geopolitics of natural resources. In the early 1970s, most of the former colonies in Southern Africa were still weak and insecure, heavily dependent—then as now—on exports of raw materials to meet their minimum needs in technology and, in some cases, in food. Few had established truly stable institutions; with a few exceptions, ruling elites were more powerful than the rule of law and constitutional procedures. Few of the nations had effective military forces, the resources to build them or, in truth, any great need for them.

While world consumption of mineral resources was relatively high because of the war in Vietnam and a high level of economic activity elsewhere, new mineral discoveries maintained or increased the level of known reserves in most of the major resources. One exception was tungsten, but that may have been from lack of information rather than lack of resources; China is a major producer of tungsten, and because of the compulsive secrecy of the Maoist regime, little was known in the outside world about the true extent of China's tungsten reserves.

By 1973, consumption of many raw materials had surged, and a worldwide shortage set off new rounds of price increases. Then from a totally different quarter came a fresh reminder of the world's vulnerability to shortages of vital raw materials. The Arab oil boycott of 1973–74 was a brutal reminder to the developed world of its critical dependence upon a few key areas for natural resources. The oil embargo and subsequent meteoric price rise had another effect: a sharp increase in the cost of energy, an essential component in the recovery, processing and transportation of raw materials.

It is not at all clear that the Soviet Union in 1975 had a well-thought-out plan to move into Southern Africa. But the collapse of the Portuguese in Mozambique and Angola at a moment when the entire Western world had suffered a major setback in the Persian Gulf and the U.S. had undergone a humiliating defeat in Vietnam opened African opportunities that must have widened the eyes of the planners in the Kremlin.

Entering upon this scene was the Soviet Union with newly acquired airlift and sealift capability and in Cuba a junior partner with a well-trained army, no concern for dissent at home and an eagerness to expand its influence in the world and in the Soviet bloc. For

Moscow, the stakes were tempting, the risk of a major confrontation with the West minimal, and the stage was set for a new era in the history of Africa.

Cuba was no newcomer to Africa in 1975. Made bold by his successful revolution and seeking a wider world stage, Fidel Castro sent a battalion of troops and other aid to help Algeria in its brief war with Morocco in 1963. Later, on the invitation of resident leftist regimes, he provided contingents of palace guards and security forces to the leaders of Guinea, Guinea-Bissau and Congo-Brazzaville. He even sent a small contingent to Congo-Leopoldville (which later became Zaire) in 1965 to join leftist insurgents fighting against the conservative Moise Tshombe, later withdrawing them after Joseph Mobutu assumed power in the fall of 1965.[4] Except in the case of Ethiopia and later Angola, the Cuban forces were relatively small, and Castro's motives not entirely clear. The Cubans served to shore up revolutionary regimes, sometimes against the more conservative forces at the head of the national military establishments, and to accumulate political IOUs to be claimed at some indeterminate time in the future. Castro has served the interest of the Soviet Union, without, however, becoming totally a pawn of Moscow.

By contrast, Moscow has avoided the dispatch of visible and identifiable contingents of Soviet troops, and has sought to keep a low military profile in Africa. An exception was in Ethiopia, where four Soviet generals headed by the then first deputy commander in chief of the Soviet ground forces coordinated the Ethiopian military offensive with the help of Soviet instructors, technicians and other support personnel.[5]

Elsewhere in Africa, the Soviets have largely limited their military role to the dispatch of advisors and to the supply of arms. But the effect of the Soviet-Cuban teamwork has been to create a Communist military presence in Africa of impressive strength and effectiveness as long as it faces only African troops of limited training and with inferior weapons. What will happen if the Cubans and their Soviet allies ever tangle openly with the well-equipped, well-trained forces from South Africa is a matter of considerable conjecture.

The presence of a well-armed Communist-led military force in Angola has renewed South Africa's deepest fears of Soviet encirclement and heightened concern at the presence of Communist-aided black South African guerrillas in Mozambique. Pretoria responded by strengthening its defense forces and its arms industry and by staging preemptive raids against guerrilla camps in Mozambique. In August 1981 South Africa staged a more sustained offensive backed by armor and air power in Angola. Its apparent purpose was to kill guerrillas and seize weapons and ammunition being provided for SWAPO guerrillas to use in Namibia. The killing of two Soviet officer-advisors and the capture of a Russian warrant officer in Angola seemed to the South Africans to validate their concern at the growing Soviet-inspired threat to their security.

Just what are the Soviet aims in Africa? As the authors of one study put it, there are as many lists of Soviet objectives as there are Western analysts studying them. These authors, one of whom, Chester A. Crocker, was later appointed assistant secretary of state for African affairs, rate the Soviet objectives in this order:

• To establish a strong and irreversible Soviet presence as a major force to be reckoned with and as an accepted part of the African terrain.

• To create a climate in which African states will develop along the Soviet model rather than as politically free governments oriented toward the market economy.

• To diminish Western influence in Africa as a precondition for further Soviet advances on the continent.

• To limit the influence of China, which has enjoyed a reputation as a patron of black liberation movements.

• By allying itself with African causes genuinely popular among developing nations, to swing the nonaligned movement closer to Moscow.

• In raw materials, to persuade Africans to pursue nationalization actions and to insist on higher prices while obtaining for the Soviet Union the capability to practice "denial strategy" in crisis situations to put political pressure on the West.[6]

Possibly to avoid alarming the West, the Soviet Union has not established any known bases in Southern Africa for its naval and air forces, though its ships call in the ports of friendly countries and its aircraft use the major airports, in particular the one at Luanda, the capital of Angola. From there, long-range Soviet aircraft are believed to maintain surveillance over Western ship movements in the South Atlantic.

While any attempt to interfere with Western shipping would be an act of war and likely to bring instant retaliation, if war should erupt elsewhere the Soviet presence in Southern Africa could become a serious threat to Western ships carrying oil from the Persian Gulf and strategic minerals from Southern Africa. The Soviet Navy, its strength multiplied under the leadership of one of the world's authentic naval geniuses, Admiral Gorshkov, is believed to have the capability to interdict the sea routes around the Cape of Good Hope. Prudent Western planners must assume that such an attempt would be made in any general war.

Meanwhile, the Soviets and their friends are well placed to cut off some supplies of critical materials almost at will and without directly involving the Soviet Union. The copper belt of Zaire and Zambia, source of most of the Western world's cobalt, is vulnerable to guerrilla raids, as was demonstrated in 1978.

Further, Gabon, a small country on the west coast of Africa, is the source of nearly half of the manganese ore used in the U.S. The Gabonese ore is shipped by rail through the Marxist country of Congo-Brazzaville to the port of Pointe Noire for loading aboard ships. The Congolese government earns useful foreign exchange for the shipping and handling of this ore, and in the past has expedited its movement. The port of Pointe Noire is only a few miles from the Angolan enclave of Cabinda, where American-operated oil wells are guarded by Cuban troops, but where a separatist movement, working for the secession of Cabinda from Angola, is also smoldering. A risk to the manganese ore from Gabon could arise from any of several developments: a political decision by the Congolese under pressure from the Soviets to cut it off, a guerrilla raid from Marxist Angola or even sabotage of the rail line by the non-Communist separatists of Cabinda. At this writing, it appears to be in everyone's interest to keep the manganese moving. How long that fortunate condition will prevail is anyone's guess.

Meanwhile, the Soviet Union has established a network of commercial agreements throughout Africa. By the end of 1977, Moscow had established formal economic assistance projects in 27 African countries. Under one such agreement, in Congo-Brazzaville, the Soviet Union brought on stream in 1980 a lead and zinc mining operation expected to produce some 30,000 tons of concentrate a year. Elsewhere, Soviet and COMECON experts are conducting geophysical and geological surveys for the discovery of other resources.

Any mines developed as a result of these explorations clearly will be operated under the Soviet model for state enterprises rather than along Western commercial lines. Daniel Fine has pointed out numerous flaws and rigidities that impede the efficient operation of these state enterprises. In the Soviet Union, division of responsibility between the ministries for ferrous and nonferrous metals has been a surprising obstacle to the efficient development of multimineral deposits. Beyond that, a preoccupation with production quotas as a measure of management performance leads some mine managers to work out their highest-grade ores for maximum quick production rather than for long-term efficiency.[7]

Whatever the defects of the Soviet management system, the trend in Southern Africa in pro-Soviet countries and others is to develop mineral resources through state-controlled enterprises rather than through commercial companies or "foreign monopolies," in the Soviet terminology. Growing state control will lend itself to the cartelization of minerals, the control of markets and prices by international networks of producers.

In Southern Africa, the Soviets have sought to overcome their chronic shortage of hard currency (in other words, U.S. dollars) by developing barter. They have traded machinery, aircraft, power equipment, trucks, mining machinery and railroad rolling stock for minerals and other commodities. The Soviet Union offers a large market for the tropical fruits and other agricultural products that are supplied to much of the West from Latin America and Asia. The expanding pattern is one in which barter effectively replaces cash transactions, serving to exclude Western consumers from critical and strategic materials except on Soviet terms.

That is one definition of a Resource War.

7

Submarine Wealth: Who Owns the Bottom of the Sea?

Far out in the depths of the deep blue sea, beyond the reach of shore-based cannon and traditional maritime law, lies one of the world's great treasures in metallic ores. Black potato-shaped nodules resting on the bottom of the sea two to four miles beneath the sunlight contain enough manganese, nickel, copper and cobalt to meet the world's needs for decades to come. Engineers backed by multinational corporations have devised recovery methods that appear to be practical and economic. But the seabed rocks have become the prize in a fierce political and ideological struggle between the developed and the developing worlds. Until that struggle is resolved, the nodules will likely remain at the bottom of the deep blue sea, and the world will continue to look to land-based mines for its manganese, nickel, copper and cobalt.

In an earlier era, the seabed minerals would have belonged to anyone with the foresight and resources to recover them. But a seemingly innocuous resolution adopted by the General Assembly of the United Nations created a new claim on behalf of "all mankind" to the resources at the bottom of the sea. That resolution, adopted without a dissenting vote on December 17, 1970, declared that:

> The sea-bed and the ocean floor . . . beyond the limits of national jurisdiction . . . are the common heritage of mankind . . . and no State shall claim or exercise sovereignty or sovereign rights over any part thereof.

In the years since 1970, the nations of the Third World—generally defined as all those outside the Western industrial group and Japan, and outside the Soviet bloc of Eastern Europe—have seized upon the U.N. resolution to stake a claim to the seabed minerals.

They fought with tenacity and skill to establish their claim, and while they are very far from mining the seabed with their own men and machines, they are intent upon extracting the highest possible price from the industrial nations with the ability and need to do so. This struggle has been fought out in the long-running United Nations Conference on the Law of the Sea, or UNCLOS in its official acronym. In 1982, the eventual outcome was unpredictable, but the very nature of the struggle seemed to make one point clear: no one is likely to gain any great benefit from the seabed minerals in the decade of the 1980s, and the outlook is scarcely more encouraging for the 1990s. The twenty-first century? Who can say?

The existence of the seabed nodules was first noted during an exploratory voyage of the British research vessel HMS *Challenger* in the years 1873 to 1876, but for decades after that the rocks remained little more than a scientific curiosity, since no one knew how to recover and refine them in volume at a manageable cost. As long as rich deposits of the same minerals were accessible on land on reasonable terms, there was little need to make the huge effort and investment necessary to mine the seabed. But a number of developments in the 1960s and 1970s made the seabed nodules increasingly attractive to private mining companies and even more attractive to strategic planners seeking secure sources for defense-related raw materials.

Industrial nations became concerned at their dependence upon a small number of primary producers of nickel, manganese and cobalt. At the same time, the countries producing these minerals developed a growing sense of the importance of the strategic prizes that they controlled, and began to devise ways to extract political leverage as well as economic return from their resources. Against this background, the industrial nations began to see the seabed minerals as a possible alternative to Third World sources.

No one, however, ever confused the minerals of the deep seabed with a free lunch. Prior to the 1970s, no one had ever devised a way to recover the seabed minerals economically and in volume. But the potential for the development of a new mineral bonanza on the bottom of the sea began to interest some powerful players. The stakes were enormous, and so was the ante to get into the game. Anyone hoping to develop a viable deep-sea mining system would have to commit around $100 million just to find out what equipment would be needed, and another $1 billion at a minimum to bring a mining venture to the point of producing its first revenue dollar.

While the men who prospected the deep sea were not strangers to economic risk, neither were they foolhardy. To spread the risk and widen the base of capital and talent available, they chose friends and allies to join in the search. In time, five major groups of companies appeared on the scene:

• Kennecott Exploration Corp., headed by the U.S.'s Kennecott Corp., and including Canada's Noranda Mines, Japan's Mitsubishi, and the British-based Rio Tinto Zinc and Consolidated Goldfields.

• Ocean Mining Associates (OMA), formed by U.S. Steel and the Pittsburgh-based Sun Oil Co. and Belgium's Union Minière.

• Ocean Management Inc. (OMI), formed by Canada's INCO, the Texas-based SEDCO, three German companies and 23 Japanese companies.

• Ocean Minerals Co. (OMC), also known as the Lockheed group, formed by the U.S.'s Lockheed Corp., Standard Oil of Indiana and Bos Kalis Westminster, a Dutch dredging company.

• Association Française pour l'Etude et la Recherche des Nodules (AFERNOD), representing French government and private interests in the fields of mining, science and nuclear power.

The consortia spent substantial funds to explore the possibilities of seabed mining and to develop the required technology. Ocean Minerals Co. alone spent $120 million to develop and test a scaled-down ocean mining system. Conrad Welling, a company executive, said that his group's overall development plan called for building a larger pilot plant at a further cost of $150 million to $200 million, then moving on to a full-production plant at the cost of another $1 billion. Given the legal uncertainties prevailing in 1982, Welling added that his companies could not hope to raise the necessary capital to proceed. Even with full financing and legal clearance, he estimated it would take his companies ten years to produce their first pound of commercial metal from the seabed.

Although the mining groups have developed a variety of engineering approaches to the problem of seabed mining, their experts are convinced that they can solve the technical problems, that they can find, recover and process the seabed minerals at costs competitive with those of land-based mines. The major obstacles are not technical but political and legal: the absence of a framework of national and international law to legitimize and protect the seabed miners and their enormous investments. "Under present circumstances," says the Lockheed group's Conrad Welling, "we could not attract capital because there is no assurance in the Law of the Sea Treaty that we would have a mine site." Marne Dubs of the Kennecott consortium agrees: "We see no possibility of considering moving ahead unless a satisfactory legal-political framework is in place." Adds Richard Greenwald of Ocean Mining Associates: "The Treaty does not promote ocean mining."

Phillips Hawkins, a U.S. Steel vice-president who formerly headed Ocean Mining Associates, argued: "The seabed, like the air we breathe, should be free to anyone who wants to use it." But the Law of the Sea negotiators have rejected this philosophy.

How did the world reach the point at which 125 or so developing countries, none with the technological ability or financial resources to mine the seabed, can hold the mineral riches of the seabed hostage? At which developed industrial nations with the need for the minerals and the ability to recover them are barred from doing so?

CANNONBALL SOVEREIGNTY

For centuries, most countries claimed a uniform territorial sea of three miles, the range of an eighteenth-century cannon shot, and considered the fish of the sea an inexhaustible resource and the oceans too vast for man to pollute. But in the years after World War II, new circumstances led to a growing demand for changes in the rules governing the seas.

The U.S. itself contributed to this trend when President Harry Truman in 1945 proclaimed the right of the U.S. to explore for gas and oil out to the edge of the continental shelf, defined as the line where the ocean depth reached 200 meters. Other nations expanded their territorial claims, and by 1973 nearly half of the world's coastal nations claimed sovereignty out to 12 miles. Some Latin American nations, in fact, extended their claims out to 200 miles, leading to the arrest of foreign fishing boats working waters their governments regarded as high seas. At the same time, the depletion of some fish stocks and the spread of maritime pollution from land and from ships forecast even more serious troubles in the years ahead unless the world could agree on a new set of rules.

The widening of the territorial seas was a matter of special concern to the U.S. and the Soviet Union. For strategic reasons, both wanted untrammeled freedom to send their merchant ships, aircraft and naval vessels, including submerged submarines, through narrow international straits. Of special importance were the straits of Gibraltar, only nine miles wide at its narrow point, and Hormuz, in the Persian Gulf, even narrower and a potential choke point for much of the West's oil from the Middle East. Any attempt to close either strait was certain to set off a dangerous international crisis.

As early as the 1960s, the U.S. and the Soviet Union met to discuss the problem of growing restrictions on navigation. They concluded that the only way to restrain other nations from widening their territorial claims over the once free seas was to call an international conference. Mineral prices were soaring, and the economic outlook for seabed mining was improving. Almost every nation in the world felt it had something to gain from the creation of a new charter for the seas. For the major powers, the prize was a fresh guarantee of navigational freedom. Smaller coastal states sought international guarantees for their legal rights, while even the inland nations with no access to the sea sought to gain a share in the resources—living and nonliving—of the bounty of the oceans. Eventually these issues and others were linked, and the Third Law of the Sea Conference met in Caracas in 1974 to start the long and difficult process of writing a charter for the oceans.

As it happened, the conference opened in the year in which the developing nations pushed their proclamation of a New International Economic Order through the U.N. General Assembly, asserting their claim to a greater share of the world's resources. They formed a bloc called the Group of 77, soon to grow to well over 100 nations, diverse in membership but cohesive in its determination to confront the rich nations in a struggle for control of the treasures in and under the oceans. They sent their best diplomats to the conference, leading Alan Beesley, Canada's senior representative, to remark, "If I were to pick out the 15 best delegates at this conference, two-thirds of them would be from developing countries." For the developing countries, the navigation issues, scientific research (in part a code for the right of the superpowers to plant submarine listening devices on the ocean floor), fisheries conservation and pollution were all secondary issues. Their primary objective was to extract the maximum possible benefit from the resources of the seabed. Skillfully they yielded to the big powers on big-power issues, bargaining doggedly on the points that mattered to them. Rules of the conference demanded few formal votes. Consensus was the key to progress. As interpreted, this meant that neither the Third World nations with their numbers nor the big powers with their economic and military might could run roughshod over the other.

"STRANGE BEDFELLOWS"

With surprising frequency the U.S. and the Soviet Union united in debate against the small Third World countries that on other occasions had seemed to the West only too willing to bend to Moscow's political will. The Soviet Union concentrated on navigational issues. This was understandable for an emerging naval and maritime power filled with determination to establish and defend its right to "unimpeded access" to the world's oceans and straits.

The USSR also voted often with the West to minimize restrictions on seabed mining. Moscow may well have anticipated the time when it may need to turn to the sea for minerals as it depletes its land-based mines. Viewing this kaleidoscope of shifting alliances led Bernardo Zuleta, a special representative of the U.N. Secretary General, to crack, "The seabed makes strange bedfellows."

In the creation of the conference's organizational structure, the Third World delegates saw one of their own installed as head of the First Committee, the body charged with drafting the treaty provisions on control and exploitation of the deep seabed. The chairman was Paul Bamela Engo of Cameroon, a onetime Olympic hop-skip-and-jump competitor, a London-trained lawyer, a distinctive figure in his tribal robe and red fez, a man with the bearing of an African chief and an ego to match. "My strategy," he once explained, "is to bully my committee into cooperation."

By the end of the second negotiating session, which was held in the Palais des Nations in Geneva in 1975, Engo and his committee had shaped a draft on seabed mining that in outline survived in the treaty draft of 1980. Under the Engo draft, 1980 version, the world's endowment of minerals in the deep seabed beyond the 200-mile Exclusive Economic Zone reserved to coastal states would be controlled by an International Seabed Authority (ISA) fashioned as a smaller replica of the United Nations itself. The ISA would consist of a large Assembly open to all U.N. members on a one-nation, one-vote basis; a governing council of 36 members; an operating arm to be known as the Enterprise; and a number of commissions with specialized functions. The Enterprise would levy assessments on member nations and assess charges against companies engaged in seabed mining. In this "parallel system," as it came to be called, the Enterprise would also function as a mining operator, competing for markets with private or state-owned ventures that the ISA would also regulate.

Under the treaty draft, four-year memberships in the governing Council would be allocated under a formula awarding 18 seats to ensure broad geographical representation; the remaining seats would be reserved for developing countries (six), mineral-exporting countries (four), mineral-consuming and -importing countries (four), and states with investments in seabed mining ventures (four). American critics complained that while the formula guaranteed a minimum of three seats to the Soviet bloc, none of the six seats earmarked for the Western industrial states was set aside for the U.S. Under this formula or anything closely resembling it, the U.S. and the West would constitute a small minority in a ruling Council dominated by Third World countries.

As negotiations ground through seven years and nine sessions in Geneva and New York, American mining executives, their friends in Congress and other U.S. observers became increasingly concerned that the Third World socialist philosophy permeating the conference would render the deep seabed and its treasures forever off limits to Western mining companies and to their governments. They were disturbed at the prospect of a top-heavy international bureaucracy exercising an iron control of the seabed minerals.

Industry observers communicated their fears to the State Department, directly to the U.S.'s Law of the Sea negotiators and to members of Congress. Some senators and representatives with constituencies in mining and fishing maintained an especially close watch on the proceedings and warned the negotiators that the U.S. Senate might well reject a treaty that failed to protect U.S. interests.

The American negotiators were able to work some improvements into the texts. On the whole, the provisions they won on navigation, maritime research, fisheries and pollution control, all matters of considerable interest to the U.S., were satisfactory. But the feeling grew that these victories were won at the expense of U.S. interests in seabed mining. The trade-off concept became a rationale for failure to meet U.S. needs in mining.

In 1980, American mining interests were far from pleased with the treaty provisions of greatest concern to them; nevertheless, the momentum of seven years of work seemed to be driving the conference toward a conclusion and a treaty. It must be a good treaty, some reasoned, since almost everybody is a little unhappy about something. In September 1980 Elliot Richardson, a Massachusetts Republican whom President Carter had appointed as chief sea-law negotiator, told the American Mining Congress that the U.S. team had negotiated 120 improvements in the seabed mining provisions. With a few further revisions, Richardson predicted, "We will then have a treaty which in my judgment, the deep seabed mining industry and American industry in general should wish to see ratified."[1]

Two months later, the American voters elected Ronald Reagan to the White House and a Republican majority to the Senate, and all bets were off on the sea treaty. In an action presaged by the 1980 Republican campaign platform ("Too much concern has been lavished on nations unable to carry out sea bed mining with insufficient attention paid to gaining early American access to it") the president announced that the U.S. would withdraw from substantive negotiations on the treaty pending a full review of its provisions by his Administration. Nearly a year later, he spelled out his objections to the treaty draft, but also insisted that if the treaty negotiators were willing to meet his objections, the U.S. would sign the treaty.

The president's objections focused upon many of the same points that the mining industry and some former senior negotiators had cited as weaknesses in the text. Reagan said he would seek a treaty:

• That *will not deter development of any deep seabed mineral resources to meet national and world demand*.

Other spokesmen explained this was an objection to draft treaty provisions placing severe limits on production by any one country or mining company, and further limiting production to protect the markets of land-based producers.

• That *would assure access to the seabed, promote the development of the resources and avoid monopolization of the resources by the operating arm of the International Seabed Authority*.

In this point, spokesmen explained, the president sought to protect the rights of "pioneer" companies that had invested heavily in seabed exploration and prevent their exclusion by the Authority for purely political or arbitrary reasons. This was the president's rejoinder to a Third World campaign to vest large powers in the International Seabed Authority to the detriment of Western and private interests. Here was a direct ideological clash: a capitalistic objection to the socialistic model the Third World attempted to set for seabed development.

• That *must provide a decision-making role in the deep seabed regime that fairly reflects and effectively protects the political and economic interests and financial contributions of participating states.*

Simply stated, this was Reagan's demand for greater protection for the rights of investing, mineral-consuming countries such as the U.S.

• That *must not allow for amendments to come into force without approval of the participating states.*

The president's target was a treaty provision calling for a revision conference to be started 15 years after the effective date of the treaty, with authority to mandate changes even over the objection of member states. In effect the president was refusing to commit the U.S. to accept future treaty changes, thus preserving the right of the Senate to "advise and consent" to all treaties binding on the U.S.

• That *must not set other undesirable precedents for international organizations.*

This responded to fears that the vastly complex sea treaty might set precedents that the U.S. would not wish to follow in other areas of international law or practice.

• That *must be likely to receive the advice and consent of the Senate.*

Provisions that would have required seabed mining companies to sell their technology to the International Seabed Authority and competing operators had met strong objections within the U.S. mining industry and within the government. Said one Administration spokesman: "There is a deeply held view in our Congress that one of America's greatest assets is its capacity for innovation and invention and its ability to produce advanced technology." The forced transfer of that technology was simply unacceptable to the U.S. Equally objectionable was a draft treaty provision calling for the full participation in the treaty not only by governments but by "national liberation movements," such as the Palestine Liberation Organization. That provision alone was termed a "treaty stopper" by some U.S. critics.

AFTER THE BOMBSHELL

The president's demands touched off a chorus of complaint from Third World representatives at the United Nations, who maintained that the U.S. was reneging on commitments made by its representatives over ten years of negotiations. But in truth, the clear terms of the negotiation provided that nothing is final until everything is final, and the president was clearly within his rights in taking his strong position. Further, almost no one with understanding of the American political system could believe that the U.S. Senate would accept the treaty in the draft form that had emerged by 1982. So the president was introducing a note of reality into the proceedings, a point that the more sophisticated Third Worlders could privately admit.

Further, the president had some impressive ammunition with which to defend his position. Without the capital and the technology of the U.S. and other major industrial powers, no one is likely to mine the deep seabed for many years—almost certainly not in the twentieth century. Further, almost all of the conference participants, including those most critical of the U.S., really wanted the world's leading economic power "on board" the treaty to establish its credibility.

Anticipating a possible deadlock on the seabed mining provisions, the U.S., along with the United Kingdom, France, Belgium, the Netherlands and Japan, worked out a fallback position to assume in the event that the broader Law of the Sea Treaty failed. This Reciprocating States Agreement, if adopted, would provide a legal framework for seabed mining should the larger treaty become hopelessly deadlocked. The president of the U.S. could approve it as an executive agreement without going through the formal ratification procedures demanded by a full treaty. U.S. legislation was adopted authorizing the licensing of U.S. companies to explore seabed sites after 1982, and providing for the licensing of seabed mining production after 1988, but only if the wider Law of the Sea convention fails to come into effect by that date.

The legal theory behind the mini-treaty maintains that prior to adoption of a general Law of the Sea convention, all nations hold inherent open-sea rights stemming from centuries of practice; any nation not signing away those rights in a new treaty would preserve all its traditional rights, including the right to mine the seabed beneath international waters. In this view, nations signing the Reciprocating States Agreement, or mini-treaty, would not be asserting new claims, merely reasserting old ones.

On April 30, 1982, the United Nations Conference on the Law of the Sea voted to adopt a treaty based on the text that had been eight years in negotiation.

At the final session of the conference, the U.S. delegate, James L. Malone, acknowledged that the final two months of bargaining had produced some "modest improvements" in the text, but not enough to win U.S. support for the treaty. He declared that the treaty as written would not encourage but would deter the development of seabed mining. More important, perhaps, was the treaty provision calling for amendment of the treaty in 20 years by three-fourths of the members, which might or might not include the U.S. This possibility of amendment without the consent of the U.S. Administration or the Senate goes against U.S. constitutional practice, and probably against the constitution itself. Mr. Malone also restated the U.S. objections to treaty provisions calling for mandatory transfer of mining technology to the Enterprise and to other nations, and to the power of the international organization to limit production and sustain prices of minerals.

In the end, 130 nations, the great majority from the Third World, voted to adopt the treaty. It will become effective when 60 members have signed and ratified it. The U.S., Turkey, Israel and Venezuela voted against adoption. The Soviet Union, along with West Germany, Great Britain and 14 other European nations, abstained.

These developments appeared to bear out a widely held view that no one is likely to engage in seabed mining on a commercial scale before 1995, if then. The outlook, in fact, for mankind to begin to recover the mineral riches of the seabed is almost as murky as on that day in 1974 when the nations of the world, in an atmosphere of hope and optimism, set out to write a charter for the seas that would win universal acceptance. That universally acceptable treaty was still far from a reality.

POLYMETALLIC SULFIDES

Since the Law of the Sea negotiations opened in 1974, fresh scientific discoveries have shed new light on the existence of undersea minerals. In the late 1970s and early 1980s, undersea explorers operating at great depth in tiny submersible craft discovered extensive mineral deposits in the form of mudlike sulfides. These minerals have formed along lines where the tectonic plates of the earth's crust have moved apart in "spreading centers," permitting superheated mineral-laden waters associated with molten rock beneath the seabed to spurt up into the cold body of the seas, precipitating deposits of sulfides of lead, zinc, copper, silver and other metals.

Unlike manganese-nickel-copper-cobalt nodules, which rarely occur within 200 miles of a major land body, sulfide deposits are being discovered well within the 200-mile economic zones of Mexico, the U.S. and Canada in the Pacific, and in the narrow waters of the Red Sea. In theory, these sulfide deposits may occur over many thousands of linear kilometers where spreading centers create the conditions for their formation.

No one has developed a process for the commercial recovery and refining of these submarine sulfide deposits, but their known existence offers the possibility that they may emerge as significant economic resources of the future. Where the sulfides occur in the deep seabed, beyond the 200-mile economic zone of any nation, their recovery would presumably be governed by provisions of any future Law of the Sea treaty or by a Reciprocating States agreement.

8

The Reagan Renaissance

Ronald Reagan ran for president in 1980 promising to rebuild America's military power. He was aware that on land, at sea, and in the air and outer space, the Soviet Union was outspending and outmanning the U.S. and its allies, tilting the balance of power dangerously in its own direction. Even before the election, Reagan and his staff began to plan how to rebuild the armed forces and the industrial base that sustains them.

In 1981, nearly a year after Reagan's election, the Department of Defense issued a report laying out many of the facts and figures on which the Administration had based its early decisions. This 99-page document, entitled *Soviet Military Power,*[1] revealed information compiled by Western intelligence services, much of it presented earlier to NATO defense ministers at a meeting in Bonn as a top-secret "threat assessment" of Soviet military power. The ministers were so impressed that they urged Secretary of Defense Caspar Weinberger to make relevant parts of the study public.

The report, illustrated with maps, drawings and photographs, described in impressive detail the Soviets' growing arsenal of tanks, artillery, ships, aircraft and missiles. It put the strength of the Soviet armed forces at 4.8 million men (versus 2 million for the U.S.). Drawings prepared from satellite photographs and other sources depicted the Soviets' new 25,000-ton Typhoon class missile submarine, a missile launch site, the Soviets' powerful new T-80 tank and the *Kirov,* the Soviet Navy's nuclear-powered missile ship.

The Soviet lead in arms had been growing rapidly. The Soviet army of 180 divisions mans 50,000 tanks and 20,000 artillery pieces. In each of the previous eight years the Soviets had built more than 1,000 fighter planes, doubling the U.S. rate of production. The Soviet Navy had assembled a powerful seagoing force of 377 nuclear- and diesel-powered submarines and 2,082 surface combat vessels and auxiliaries, prepared to project Soviet power to distant seas and sea-lanes. Altogether Moscow was spending 10 to 12 percent of its gross national product on its armed forces, versus 5.6 percent for the U.S.

The Soviets and their Warsaw Pact allies maintain a military industrial base that is the world's largest in number of facilities and physical size. The Defense Department study reported: "The Soviet Union alone produces more weapons systems in greater quantities than any other country."

"Even the United States' lead in basic military technology is presently being challenged," the report continued. "During the 1970s the Soviets have dramatically reduced the U.S. lead in virtually every important basic technology. The United States is losing its lead in key technologies, including electro-optical sensors, guidance and navigation, hydro-acoustics, optics and propulsion."

The Soviets, seeking to extend their power, have assigned 20,000 military personnel as advisors in 28 Third World countries "where they play a central role in organizing, training and penetrating client-armed forces." The purpose: "The Soviets are also seeking to develop a viable oil and strategic minerals denial strategy, either through physical disruption, market manipulation, or domination of producing or neighboring states. . . . By undermining Western ties with the oil and raw materials producers and exacerbating differences in the Western Alliance over policies toward these regions, the Soviets seek to erode both the economic health and political cohesion of the West."

The Administration's response to this evaluation was to push through Congress a $200-billion defense appropriation and to plan for a long period of sharply increased arms production. And since nearly everything in the military arsenal that flies, floats, orbits, rolls on tracks or wheels or uses electronic signals demands strategic metals, the Administration sought to assure its future sources of these materials. Its strategies called for strengthening the National Defense Stockpile, encouraging domestic production of some critical materials, removing some counterproductive government regulations from the books and making some fresh approaches in foreign policy.

Some of these steps were foreshadowed by an unusual preelection move by Ronald Reagan. He had appointed a task force of experts to advise him on policy involving strategic materials. Heading the task force was Daniel McMichael of Pittsburgh, who had organized a 1980 conference in Pittsburgh on the Resource War. Also serving on the task force were Murray Weidenbaum, an economist who had written and lectured on the negative effects of overzealous government regulation, and W. Perry Pendley, a Republican staff counsel to the House Mines and Mining subcommittee. (Both Weidenbaum and Pendley were later to serve in the Administration, Weidenbaum as chairman of the Council of Economic Advisers until August, 1982, and Pendley as deputy assistant secretary of the interior dealing with energy and minerals.) Armed with the task force's study and recommendations, the Administration was prepared to move quickly after Inauguration Day, January 20, 1981.

Soon after the new Administration took office the Defense Department launched a detailed study of the Department's future needs in critical and strategic materials, seeking to anticipate and prevent some of the bottlenecks and lost motion that had characterized the crash programs of earlier emergencies. Richard Donnelly, a Defense Department official concerned with planning for material supply, told members of a Senate subcommittee on Energy and Mineral Resources on April 9, 1981: "We, D.O.D., may require 100 pounds of cobalt to build an aircraft, but the industrial facilities building the aircraft also require cobalt for the machinery, transportation, and communications system required in the production processes. . . . Portions of the civilian economy (nondefense) must continue to function. This is accomplished through allocating a necessary quantity of a commodity to the basic industrial sector."

The Federal Emergency Management Agency, which oversees the National Defense Stockpile, receives estimates from the Defense Department on war production needs, probable shipping losses and judgments on the war "scenario." FEMA, in turn, estimates the amounts of critical materials needed to sustain the civilian economy under emergency conditions, assuming a large-scale industrial mobilization and the need to continue production for essential civilian requirements. From these estimates, and projections of domestic production of each critical material, the FEMA experts estimate the volume of each material above domestic supply needed for a three-year emergency. This constitutes the stockpile goal for each material.

As Donnelly pointed out to the Senate subcommittee, "For each pound of additional domestic capacity we can bring into production, we can reduce the stockpile goal by three pounds. Programs to stimulate domestic production capability may prove to be more cost effective than direct acquisition programs."

THE NATIONAL DEFENSE STOCKPILE

It took first the threat, then the reality of World War II to jolt the U.S. into building its first true stockpile. The prewar origins were modest enough. In 1938 the navy got an appropriation for $3.8 million to buy reserve stocks of tin, ferromanganese, tungsten ore, chromite, optical glass and manila fiber for cordage. Then on June 7, 1939, two months before the war broke out in Europe, Congress passed Public Law 76-117, the nation's first true stockpiling act, and in three appropriations gave the Treasury $70 million to buy and stockpile critical materials.

As the war in Europe flared into the 1940 blitzkrieg of the Low Countries and France, a new sense of urgency surrounded all of the U.S. war preparations. On June 25, 1940, a month after the fall of France, an alarmed Congress authorized the Reconstruction Finance Corporation to create four subsidiary corporations for specific tasks. The Rubber Reserve Co. was to buy natural rubber and set up a synthetic rubber industry. The Defense Plant Corp. was to get key war industries built. The Defense Supplies Corp. was to start buying nonminerals like medicinal drugs, cordage for the navy and kapok for life jackets, while the fourth, the Metals Reserve Co., was designated to begin stockpiling strategic minerals. One of the young executives recruited to help run the Metals Reserve Co. was Simon Strauss, a securities analyst turned government metals buyer (later he became vice-chairman of Asarco, one of the nation's major mining and smelting companies, and a spokesman for the mining and metallurgical industry).

Eventually, the Metals Reserve Co. stockpiled nearly 90 mineral products, but in 1940 it concentrated on the most urgently needed metals. The U.S. had traditionally drawn most of its tin from Southeast Asia, but in 1940 the Japanese drive into that region was threatening to cut off U.S. supplies of tin as well as natural rubber. Bolivia, the only important source of tin in the Western Hemisphere, had historically shipped its ore and concentrates to Europe for smelting.

To deal with this changing strategic situation, the Defense Plant

Corp. built a tin smelter in Texas City, Texas, and engaged a staff of Dutch metallurgical engineers to run it. At the same time, the Metals Reserve Co. quietly bought up all the tin it could find in Southeast Asia. The resulting stockpile, together with the output of the Texas smelter, met the nation's essential needs for tin throughout the war.

Before the war, the U.S. had drawn most of its aluminum from the production of the Aluminum Company of America (Alcoa) and its offshoot, the Aluminum Company of Canada (Alcan). It soon became clear to the American war planners that the aircraft factories and other war plants would need far more aluminum than existing plants could produce. The Defense Plant Corp. enlisted the help of Alcoa to design new plants and then, to avoid conflict with antitrust laws, contracted with other firms to run them. Two of these war-spawned companies became Kaiser Aluminum and Reynolds Metals, future competitors of Alcoa.

The U.S. was eager to expand aluminum capacity in Canada as well, but could not legally finance construction of new plants outside the U.S. Roosevelt's young tigers soon devised a solution to that problem. They contracted with Alcan to produce 1.7 billion pounds of aluminum—an enormous purchase at that time—and gave Alcan a down payment against future deliveries to enable the Canadian company to build new plants from the ground up.

Before the U.S. entered the war, ships carrying bauxite ore moved freely from Guiana in South America to North American ports, but after December 7, 1941, German U-boat skippers took deadly aim on these vessels carrying the raw material for the warplanes of the future, sinking nearly one-fourth of the fleet. The surviving ships pushed through with enough bauxite to meet essential needs.

Long before the war, the U.S. Steel Corp. had developed manganese mines in the interior of Brazil, moving the ore by river barges to the coast and then by ship to U.S. smelters. Although Brazil even then was beginning to restrict manganese exports, it allowed the traffic to continue through the war. Submarines picked off some of the ore ships, but the surviving ships plus others bringing manganese from India, South Africa and Cuba supplied the U.S. steel mills all through the war.

Nickel was a different problem. Much of the Free World's nickel, then as now, originated around Sudbury, Ontario, near the shores of

Lake Huron and easily accessible to the U.S. market. But Washington planners were uneasy at the nation's heavy dependence upon a single source, which conceivably could have been sabotaged. Seeking an alternate source, they had a special treaty drafted with Cuba to allow the U.S. to develop a mine on a property called Nicaro, while Freeport Sulphur, a U.S. corporation, built a nickel smelter nearby to produce metal from ore. Forty years later, that same mine and smelter, long since nationalized by Fidel Castro, are still producing nickel, but mainly for the Soviet Union and the COMECON bloc of Eastern Europe.

In copper, another key war material, the U.S. was largely self-sufficient before the war, and the copper of Peru and Chile went mostly to European markets. After the war cut off those markets, the Peruvian and Chilean producers were happy to sell their copper under long-term contracts to the U.S.-British purchasing commission, at essentially prewar prices. As the war progressed, inflation pushed up the cost of operating the mines and of everything the producing countries imported, but the U.S. and British purchasers refused to increase the contract price for copper. Prices remained low throughout the war. The arrangement irritated the Chileans and Peruvians, who were convinced that American interests were profiteering at their expense. Such irritations are durable, and these may have contributed to later political decisions to nationalize American-owned mines in Chile and Peru.

As the war progressed, the U.S. struggled to keep China fighting against Japan. The armies of Chiang Kai-shek, isolated deep in the interior of their own country, were in desperate need of supplies of all kinds, and so were the U.S. fighter squadrons based there to support Chiang's efforts. To transport high-priority cargoes to Chiang and its own airmen in China, the U.S. organized an airlift over the hump of the Himalayas. Some of the supplies thus flown perilously between the peaks in unpressurized aircraft were shipped by sea to India, but other cargoes were flown all the way from the U.S.

This air route ran from the East Coast to Puerto Rico, to Georgetown, Guiana; to Natal or Belem in Brazil, across the South Atlantic to Senegal on the hump of Africa, through Nigeria to Iraq, to Karachi in what is now Pakistan, and across India and over the world's highest mountains to Kunming, China.

For the return trip, aircraft that would otherwise have flown empty were loaded with tin, tungsten, tung oil and hog bristles from China and precious mica from India. Depending upon priorities, the returning aircraft sometimes saved cargo space to be filled in Brazil with quartz crystals for radio transmitters, and beryllium, tantalum and columbium for the Manhattan Project, which turned out the first A-bombs.

Thanks to a number of circumstances, the U.S. fought World War II without suffering militarily from major shortages of raw materials. This was due in part to prudent and early stockpiling and production planning, but it owed even more to the fact that the U.S. and its allies were able to maintain access to the mineral resources of Africa, much of Asia, Australia and Latin America all through the war.

After the war, the Congress was convinced of the necessity to create a permanent National Defense Stockpile, and through the 1950s the lawmakers provided funding for large purchases of strategic materials at prices that later looked very cheap. But in the early 1960s political and economic considerations began to play an increasing though unadmitted role in the government's stockpiling policies.

By the time John Kennedy became president, the stockpile inventories had climbed to about half of the official goals, although neither goals nor inventories were publicly disclosed at the time. President Kennedy, with his own ideas on national goals and priorities, concluded that the stockpile had become too big and too expensive. His appointees began to trim stockpile goals and to sell metals painfully accumulated since the end of World War II. In succeeding years, all the aluminum in the stockpile was sold, as was all the nickel, all the copper, most of the zinc and about half the lead. By 1964 the stockpile had accumulated about 100 million pounds of cobalt. The goal was reduced, and the surplus put on the market. Close to 60 million pounds of cobalt were sold off between 1964 and 1976. In the six months from July to December 1969, 6.5 million pounds of cobalt was sold for an average price of about $3 a pound.[2]

After taking office in January 1981, the Reagan Administration launched a new review of stockpile policy. In its semiannual report dated March 31, 1981, FEMA valued its then-current inventory of materials at $12.56 billion (original cost: $3.5 billion). But because of changing goals, $4.92 billion of the stockpile was represented by materials in excess of goals, while the cost of a stockpile meeting all goals was estimated then at $20.14 billion. To put it more simply, if the stockpile agency could realize $4.92 billion on the sale of surplus material, it would need all of those funds plus another $7.58 billion to build the stockpile to its stated goals, assuming no increases in the price of materials.

The maintenance of a $20-billion stockpile is a heavy burden, particularly when it must be financed at double-digit interest rates. The stockpile does not have a large and enthusiastic constituency lobbying for its appropriations, as do many social programs and even the national defense establishment. President Reagan recognized the practical difficulties of finding $8 billion to bring the stockpile up to its full goals, but within a few weeks of his inauguration he ordered the first major additions to the stockpile in 20 years. On March 13, 1981, the president said: "It is now widely recognized that our nation is vulnerable to sudden shortages in basic raw materials that are necessary to our defense production base."

He ordered the stockpile administrators to give priority to the purchase of 13 materials, including cobalt, columbium, aluminum oxide, nickel, platinum group metals, tantalum and vanadium. He assigned the highest priority to cobalt and directed the purchase of 5.2 million pounds.

To help finance these purchases, the stockpile administrators proposed to sell off surpluses of several materials and to dispose of the entire inventory of silver, 139.5 million ounces. Roy Markon, commissioner of the Federal Property Resources Services and the official in charge of sales and purchases for the stockpile, argued for the silver sale: "We do not have silver missiles or silver bullets in our arsenals. It is far more important for us to have adequate supplies of cobalt, chromium, manganese or titanium than it is for us to maintain excess stocks of silver in our inventory."[3]

Congressmen from silver-mining states resisted the liquidation of the silver stockpile, and *Barron's*, the New York financial journal, argued editorially against the sale on the ground of silver's importance as a strategic metal. Eventually, a legislative compromise was reached authorizing the sale of $535 million ounces of silver in fiscal 1982, representing at late 1981 prices about half the silver in the stockpile, and further sales in later years. However, because of falling silver prices and possibly because of protests from silver producers, the GSA sold only two million ounces in the first year this policy was in effect.

Experts inside and outside the government have argued that the stockpile agency should be authorized to use the proceeds of such sales to purchase more urgently needed materials, in effect at the discretion of the president. But Congress has resisted delegating control of stockpile purchases, and every appropriation for the stockpile still has to be cleared through the legislative process. Because of the large sums of money involved, and the conflicting interests between producers who seek high prices and consumers who are constantly eyeing the stockpile as a source of cheap raw materials, it is doubtful if stockpile policies can very soon be removed from politics.

THE INTERIOR VIEW

Domestic economic and regulatory policy must be adjusted to remove impediments to the greater development of our own energy and raw material resources.
—Republican Platform, 1980

In December 1980 when President-elect Reagan was putting together a new administration, he summoned a Denver lawyer whom he had never met to call upon him at Blair House to discuss a possible appointment as secretary of the interior. James Watt had earned a reputation as a Western free-enterprise activist, speaking and litigating against what he and his Mountain States Legal Foundation regarded as the dead hand of Washington bureaucracy on the vast expanses of federal lands. He was also no stranger to the mazes of bureaucratic Washington, having headed the Interior Department's Bureau of Outdoor Recreation in the Nixon and Ford Administrations.

How, the president-elect asked his visitor, did Watt propose to help him carry out his campaign commitment to increase domestic mining production and reduce U.S. reliance on imported strategic metals? Watt was ready to tick off a program of action for Reagan. He would open far more of the public lands for multiple use, for mining and drilling, lumbering and grazing, as well as for recreation. He would develop a strategic minerals policy worked out in cooperation with heads of other departments and agencies. And he would try to restore the prestige and morale of the department's corps of professionals—geologists, physicists, engineers—who had felt abandoned by the previous Administration's antidevelopment mind-set.

The interview stretched from a scheduled 15 minutes to half an hour. When it was over, the president-elect had found a secretary of the interior, and the department was about to get its most controversial boss since Franklin Roosevelt's Harold Ickes.

In many countries, the minister of the interior is the nation's top police and security officer, but in the U.S. the secretary of the interior is the principal overseer of the public lands. He is in charge of 768 million acres—one-third of the nation's land area—owned by the federal government. Much of this land is set aside for national parks, game preserves, national forests and wilderness areas; because of this and because the Fish and Wildlife Service resides in Interior, the department finds a natural constituency among sportsmen, outdoorsmen and environmentalists. Secretary James Watt likes to point out that he is the nation's chief environmental officer.

The secretary is also the overseer of the nation's mineral resources. The Bureau of Mines, the U.S. Geological Survey and the Office of Surface Mining, Reclamation and Enforcement are all part of his domain. The secretary is thus the chief rulemaker for the exploration and development of the public lands. In part because of its divergent and often conflicting constituencies, the Department of the Interior has been a battleground in recent years between those who wish to minimize mineral development and keep the public lands pristine, and those who see these lands as a resource to be developed in the interest of economic growth and national security.

In the view of Watt, previous Administrations had tilted the balance in Interior toward environmental concerns and against the development of public lands. He was determined to shift the balance back toward development, without, he insisted, abandoning environmental concerns. As he told an audience of Associated Press editors in Toronto, "These are my priorities: to protect the environment, to create jobs, and to help strengthen the national security."[4] It was a pronouncement that might well have come from his environmental-minded predecessor, Cecil Andrus, but in Watt's voice it foretold change that would arouse the fury of members of the Sierra Club, the Audubon Society, the Wilderness Society and even the League of Women Voters.

James Watt is a man who invites controversy and appears to relish a public brawl. As Watt recalls it, he told the president-elect at their Blair House meeting, "I know I will bring controversy to your Administration. To carry out the program I have outlined here will create tremendous conflict."[5] It was an accurate forecast.

Watt rarely bothers to blunt the sharp edges of his pronouncements with a politician's diplomacy. He criticizes his predecessor, Cecil Andrus, for lack of concern with strategic metals. He shouts back at hecklers who rise to challenge him at public meetings. He is also a cartoonist's dream, with shining head, thick eyeglasses and a broad grin that becomes fixed before a hostile audience.

The secretary's appearance in Denver on September 28, 1981, to speak to the American Mining Congress set off an altogether familiar chain of events. When Watt arrived at Currigan Hall, the building was surrounded by demonstrators carrying anti-Watt signs and shouting insults at the secretary. Inside the hall, as the secretary prepared to speak, one heckler who had somehow obtained convention credentials rose to shout at the man at the podium. Another intruder pulled a paper from his pocket and began reading his own speech. Watt paused, and when the building's security officers had ejected the hecklers, he remarked, "I find it hard to have an intellectual exchange with people who only shout 'Dump Watt.'" Outside, other demonstrators set up a rhythmic cry and pounded on the doors and windows of the hall.

Watt told the mining executives that as steward of one-third of the nation's land area, he would seek "to remove impediments to the greater development of our energy and raw material resources [so that] resource access will assume an important place in economic and defense planning."

The secretary said that he had been instructed by the president to increase domestic mining production for the purpose of reducing dependence upon imported raw materials. He said that as head of the Cabinet-level Council on Natural Resources and the Environment, he would work for the development of a comprehensive strategic minerals policy: "We need a strategic minerals policy and we are determined to bring it into existence."

The Bureau of Land Management is reviewing rules and regulations governing mineral exploration on 341 million acres of land under the Bureau's control. Some 1.5 million acres previously set aside as wilderness had been judged unsuitable for that designation and would be opened to prospecting and mineral development. In Alaska, the status of 100 million acres of potentially rich mineral areas was being reviewed with the possibility of opening it to prospectors. Elsewhere, the secretary said, the department was reviewing environmental and health and safety regulations that had hampered mining operations in the U.S. without producing comparable benefits for the public health and safety.

In one important area, the department has no intention of changing the ground rules. "Friends," said the secretary, "if you are working on a proposal to mine in national parks, save your energy. It is not going to happen. Congress has set those lands aside to be preserved for generations to come and that is the way they will be managed."

Back in Washington, other Department of Interior officials add touches to the secretary's broad strokes. One expert says the department intends to end regulations that made exploration difficult even on public lands nominally open to prospecting and mining. In one wilderness area that seemed reasonably promising for minerals, prospecting parties were prohibited from flying in helicopters to remote areas. Instead, they took pack animals up into the hills until an environmental group complained that the donkeys were littering the landscape with their droppings. The prospectors tried to fit diaperlike canvas bags to their animals, but when this proved impractical, they abandoned their search.

The 1964 Wilderness Act allowed a 20-year grace period for mineral exploration before placing designated wilderness acres off limits to prospecting. For most of those 20 years, antiexploration policies by successive Administrations discouraged prospecting, even though the geology of some of the wilderness areas seemed reasonably promising for mineral discoveries. In 1982, an Administration-sponsored bill was introduced into the House of Representatives to bar most mineral exploration in wilderness areas until the year 2000, after which the policy would be reviewed. However, the bill included provisions to permit certain types of exploration in the interim. The new mineral plan, said the president in a message to Congress, "recognizes the vast, unknown and untapped mineral wealth of America and the need to keep the public's land open to appropriate mineral exploration and development." Further, said the president, "This policy is responsive to America's need for measures to diminish minerals vulnerability by allowing private enterprise to preserve and expand our minerals and materials economy."

The president's minerals plan instantly drew the fire of the National Wildlife Federation and other conservationist groups. In 1982, the ultimate shape of public policy in this area was far from clear.

Of all the publicly held lands with potential for mineral development, none seems more promising than the great expanse of Alaska, where prospecting has been prohibited or discouraged by past policies. The state of Alaska's Division of Geological and Geophysical Surveys reports the presence of economic or near-economic reserves of ten critical and strategic minerals within the state: cobalt, nickel, tin, platinum-group metals, asbestos, mercury, fluorine, tungsten, antimony and chromite.[6]

The details of the Administration's moves to open up certain public lands to controlled exploration for critical metals are less significant than its overall commitment to remove extraneous roadblocks and find to what degree the nation can reduce its dependence on foreign suppliers. Almost no one is hopeful of turning up enormous deposits on the scale of those that dot the map of Southern Africa, but even a few finds of moderate size could help protect the U.S. against crippling supply interruptions and thus strengthen its defenses and its peacetime economy.

There is a clear public interest in preserving large expanses of public lands for the enjoyment of future generations of nature lovers. There is also a clear public interest in protecting the nation against shortages of desperately needed critical materials. Threading a way through those sometimes conflicting interests is one of the sensitive political problems facing the Reagan Administration—and in all probability its successors as well.

9

The Strategic Metals

In the preceding chapters and those to follow, reference is made to many critical and strategic metals, their sources and their uses. While stocks of many of the metals discussed are held in the federal government's strategic stockpile, others that may in the future prove to be equally vital have not been earmarked for stockpiling. For some of these nonstockpiled metals, new research in the fields of metallurgy, chemistry, electronics, solar energy and weaponry is developing new uses that may lead in the future to vastly increased demand for specific elements.

Indium, gallium, germanium, rhenium and lithium, for example, are finding increasing uses in advanced, proven technology; these metals are also the subject of intense research into new applications. They merit the attention of the investor for their future potential as well as their present value. Any future decision to stockpile these relatively rare metals could have an immediate effect on markets and prices.

Germanium and indium have important applications in weapons technology. Both are employed in infrared devices used to guide the latest generation of air-to-air and ground-to-air missiles to heat-radiating aircraft. Infrared guidance systems cannot be jammed by electronic interference, a key to their military effectiveness. Both metals are also used in night sights for tanks. The Soviet Union and China have ceased exporting indium, presumably to conserve their available supplies for their military forces.

Germanium, indium and gallium all have many uses in electronics, and all may find increasing demand in the field of fiber optics, a technology permitting the transmission of television and other signals by light beams traveling through glass fibers rather than by electronic signals carried by copper wires. Fiber optic technology offers security against unauthorized tapping of signals, and great saving in weight and volume from the copper wires used in the past. New breakthroughs in this highly promising field of communications are likely.

In an era of soaring energy costs, much research is devoted to the development of cheap electric energy from sunlight. One writer, Ben Bova, author of *The High Road*,[1] foresees the development of giant solar collectors assembled in space, orbiting the earth and transmitting electricity by microwave to earth stations. Even if this development is several decades in the future, as it probably is, other solar power applications seem likely to expand future demand for such elements as indium, gallium, germanium, cadmium and possibly others.

The energy crunch is stimulating demand for yet another obscure metal, rhenium, which is useful as a catalyst in the production of the low-lead, high-octane gasoline that is much in demand since the use of lead additives to improve octane has been restricted. Rhenium is also useful in X-ray machines and in thermocouples, and it may find additional future demand in superalloys for jet engine turbine blades.

Interest grows in yet another high-technology metal, lithium. The use of lithium improves the efficiency of electrolytic cells producing aluminum, and so conserves precious energy. Lithium also holds some promise as the key element in long-life, lightweight storage batteries that may make battery-powered automobiles practical for daily use.

Other metals are of major importance to the world not because they are rare but because they are essential to key industrial processes and are found in commercial quantities in only a few areas of the world. Manganese and chromium are the prime examples. Manganese is found in great abundance in South Africa, chromium in South Africa and Zimbabwe, and both metals are also produced in the Soviet Union.

Manganese and chromium are mined as raw ores, then smelted into concentrated forms, ferromanganese and ferrochromium. In the past, producing countries routinely shipped raw ore to the U.S., where it was smelted in American furnaces using American coal and labor. In recent years, both South Africa and Zimbabwe have developed their own processing industries, using their abundant coal and cheap labor to produce a higher-grade material than raw ore. This processing of ores near the sources saves shipping costs because smaller tonnages are moved for long distances.

This transfer of processing "upstream," however, has led to a decline in U.S. smelting facilities and to greater dependence upon sources that can provide ferroalloys rather than just ore. It also raises questions about the real value of low-grade ores held in the stockpile; if smelting facilities are not available, these low-grade stockpiled ores could not readily be converted to a usable form in an emergency. All of these factors place a special premium on the stockpiling of higher-grade ferroalloys rather than raw ores.

Following are brief profiles of some of the more important critical and strategic metals:

ALUMINUM (Al)

Aluminum is a silvery metal, an excellent conductor of heat and electricity. Treated and alloyed, it has great strength in relation to its weight. It is the most abundant of the structural metals in the earth's crust, but commercial-grade deposits of bauxite ore are relatively rare, and the U.S. imports more than 90 percent of the bauxite and processed alumina used to make the primary metal.

About 20 percent of the aluminum consumed in the U.S. goes into construction, 20 percent for vehicles and transportation, 21 percent for containers and packaging and 10 percent for the electrical and communications industries. Aluminum has long been used in automobiles and its consumption there is rising as car makers strive for light weight and fuel economy. About 41 percent of the weight of a B-1 bomber is aluminum alloy. Aluminum's use in power transmission has increased to the point where it has almost displaced copper as the preferred metal for high-tension power lines.

The four largest producers of bauxite are Australia, Guinea, Jamaica and Surinam. All of these countries are significant suppliers of bauxite or alumina or both to the U.S., which uses them to produce aluminum metal in areas where electric power is cheap and plentiful.

The producer price of aluminum moved from an average of 29¢ a pound in 1970 to about 71.5¢ in 1980. In mid-1982, the dealer price was around 41¢ a pound.

Stockpile dependence and import position: Total stockpile goal in March 1981 for all forms of aluminum including bauxite, alumina, alumina metal and three grades of abrasives was 7,150,000 short tons of contained aluminum; inventory stood at 3,444,064 short tons. The U.S. imported 4 percent of its aluminum metal in 1981, but the

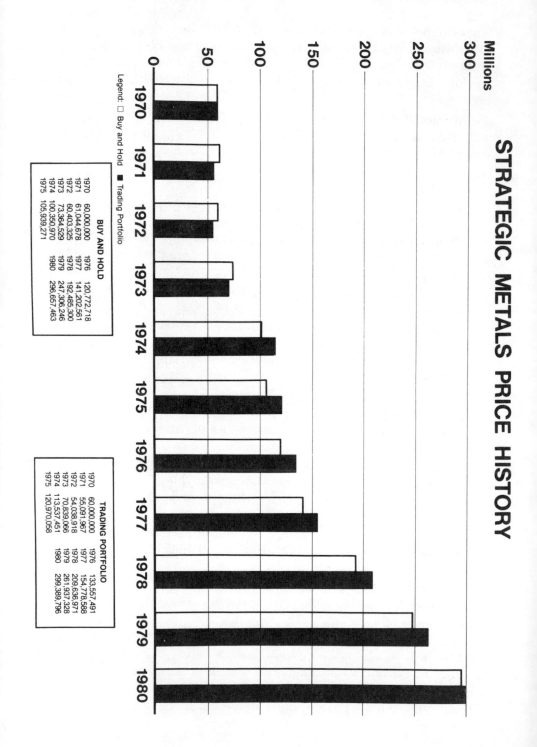

STRATEGIC METALS PRICE HISTORY

Millions

300 —
250 —
200 —
150 —
100 —
50 —
0 —

1970 1971 1972 1973 1974 1975 1976 1977 1978 1979 1980

Legend: □ Buy and Hold ■ Trading Portfolio

BUY AND HOLD

1970	60,000,000	1976	120,772,718
1971	61,044,678	1977	141,202,561
1972	60,403,325	1978	192,485,300
1973	73,364,529	1979	247,306,246
1974	100,350,970	1980	296,667,463
1975	105,939,271		

TRADING PORTFOLIO

1970	60,000,000	1976	133,557,491
1971	55,091,967	1977	154,778,588
1972	54,038,918	1978	209,636,971
1973	70,839,066	1979	261,937,328
1974	113,537,451	1980	299,389,796
1975	120,970,058		

more significant fact is that it imported 94 percent of the raw materials from which the metal was produced.

ANTIMONY (Sb)

Antimony, a silvery white metal well known in the ancient world and used as an eyebrow darkener and medication, takes its name from the Greek words *anti* and *monos,* meaning roughly "a metal seldom found alone." Its principal modern-day use is as an alloy to harden the lead used in automobile batteries; it is also used to harden lead for bullets and to make tracer bullets. It is a component of type metal and solders, and in chemical combination forms an excellent compound for flameproofing fabrics and rubber.

The U.S. produces only about 8 percent of the antimony it consumes, but recovers quite a bit from the salvage of batteries and type metals. As the Greek-based name of the metal suggests, antimony is usually found in ores in combination with other metals, and it is produced mostly as a by-product of lead and silver mines.

The U.S. imports antimony from Bolivia, China, Mexico and South Africa, and consumes about 30 percent of the total world production of the metal. U.S. consumption is expected to rise at a rate of 3 percent per annum for the rest of this century.

Since 1970 the market price for antimony has ranged from 59¢ to $2 a pound. In 1981 it was selling at around $1 a pound.

Stockpile position and import dependence: The strategic stockpile has a goal of 36,000 tons of antimony and an inventory of 40,730 tons. Import dependence was 51 percent in 1981.

BERYLLIUM (Be)

Until after World War II, beryllium was a little-known and little-used metal, but postwar research led to the discovery of a variety of uses in electronics and in the nuclear, missile and aerospace fields. Alloyed with copper, beryllium makes durable spring-type switches with many uses in electronic and electrical equipment. Aerospace uses account for about 18 percent of U.S. consumption. Beryllium is used in the manufacture of high-strength nonsparking tools, in springs, tubes and diaphragms for a wide variety of measuring instruments.

Until 1970 the U.S. was almost wholly dependent upon foreign sources for beryllium, but with the opening of mining of bertrandite in Utah, it has become largely self-sufficient in the metal. Other producing countries are Argentina, Brazil and the USSR. Because the dust of beryllium ores and compounds is highly toxic and possibly cancer-causing, special care must be exercised in mining and processing.

In the early 1970s the price of beryllium was stable at about $60 a pound; since 1976 it has risen to $120 a pound, falling to $52 in mid-1982.

Stockpile position and import dependence: The stockpile goal was revised in 1980 to 1,220 short tons of contained beryllium metal in beryl ore, beryllium-copper alloy and beryllium metal. The inventory in March 1981 was 1,061 short tons of contained metal. Import dependence in 1980 was 22 percent.

CADMIUM (Cd)

Cadmium is a silver-white soft metal recovered as a by-product of zinc smelting. It is widely used for coating and plating other metals, since it can be deposited electrically or mechanically, evenly and swiftly. It is used in the manufacture of nickel-cadmium and silver-cadmium batteries, which have a long life and high reliability over a broad range of temperatures. Paints, pigments and the manufacture of plastic and synthetic products account for most of the remaining consumption of cadmium.

There are no ores mined exclusively for cadmium, so production is not directly responsive to changes in demand. Cadmium recovery from zinc ores ranges from 1.5 kilograms to 4 kilograms of cadmium for each ton of slab zinc recovered. Some zinc ores are too poor in cadmium to justify the separate recovery of the by-product metal. Cadmium is highly toxic and must be handled with extreme care.

The price of cadmium varied widely during the 1970s, from $3.57 a pound at the start of the decade to $4.09 in 1974 to $2.76 in 1979. In mid-1982 the price stood at 75¢ a pound.

Stockpile position and import dependence: The stockpile goal for cadmium is 11,204 tons; inventory stands at 2,871 tons. Import dependence is about 63 percent. Canada, Mexico and Australia are the principal foreign sources for cadmium imports into the U.S.

CHROMIUM (Cr)

Chromium, a lustrous steel-gray metal, is one of modern industry's most useful and versatile elements and one of the most important of the critical and strategic materials. Small amounts of chromium harden steel and make it resistant to corrosion and wear. A chromium content of 4 percent or more produces stainless steel; variations in the manufacturing processes result in specialty steels suitable for such applications as surgical instruments, chemical and food processing equipment and automobile mufflers and tailpipes.

Other alloy steels can be made without chromium, but at a sacrifice in performance and cost. There is no substitute for chromium in stainless steel. Chromium is also used in the manufacture of nonferrous alloys, in chemical applications and for heat-resistant refractories in iron and steel processing.

The U.S. has no known deposits of chromium ore rich enough to sustain commercial mining, and the only domestic source of chromium is the small tonnage recovered each year for the recycling of stainless steel. It is a geological oddity that 99 percent of the world's resources of chromium are located in the Eastern Hemisphere, principally in South Africa, Zimbabwe and the Soviet Union. The USSR, an important supplier of chromium to the U.S. in the 1940s, embargoed sales to the U.S. at the time of the Korean War and did not resume shipments for ten years; since then it has met a small share of U.S. demand. South Africa and Zimbabwe are both seeking to process a greater proportion of their chromite ore into the more highly refined ferrochrome. Both countries have abundant supplies of energy (coal) near their mines, and the processing of the chromite near the mines makes a good deal of economic sense. But this pattern could lead to a withering away of U.S. facilities for smelting ferrochrome and to increasing dependence upon foreign sources for that most vital of industrial raw materials.

The price of electrolyte chromium rose from \$2,065 a metric ton in 1970 to \$9,300 a ton in 1977; in mid-1982 the dealer price stood at \$4,250 a metric ton.

Stockpile position and import dependence: The stockpile goal in March 1981 stood at 1,353,000 short tons of contained metal in five different grades of chromite plus chromium metal; the inventory stood at 1,173,230 short tons of contained chromium. Import dependence in 1981 was 90 percent.

COBALT (Co)

Cobalt is a silvery gray metal used to harden steel into heat-resistant parts for jet aircraft engines and for highly durable cutting tools. Its magnetic qualities make it useful in electrical and electronic equipment, and cobalt compounds are widely used in paints and chemicals.

Cobalt is usually found in combination with copper or nickel, and two-thirds of the world's supply of cobalt originates in the copper-cobalt mines of Zaire and Zambia. In this politically unstable region, mine production has been seriously interrupted twice in recent years by guerrilla actions, with resulting sharp price rises. The long rail links from African mines to seaports are also subject to politically related interruptions, and in 1978 and 1979 much of Zaire's mine output of cobalt was moved by air to world markets. Other sources of cobalt include Canada (where it is recovered as a by-product of nickel), Finland and Cuba. The USSR is a net importer of cobalt and therefore, in the broader sense, in competition with Western consumers for available supplies.

The U.S. recovers about 6 percent of its cobalt requirements by recycling, but otherwise is heavily dependent upon African sources for its supply. A number of small cobalt deposits have been identified in the U.S.; these may be brought into production in time with the help of government purchase programs. U.S. demand for cobalt is expected to rise by 2.5 percent a year for the rest of this century. Large supplies of cobalt are known to exist in the form of nodules on the floor of the oceans, but commercial recovery of these resources is unlikely to become a market factor before the 1990s, if then (see Chapter 7).

The price of cobalt has fluctuated wildly within the past decade, reflecting real and threatened shortages that alarmed users. The metal sold for $2.20 a pound in the early 1970s, rose as high as $25 a pound in producer contracts in 1980, and eased to the range of $9.50 in 1982 as world metal prices softened in a widespread business recession.

Stockpile position and import dependence: Cobalt is a highly important critical material because of its uses in jet aircraft, computers, communications and in mining and drilling machinery. The stockpile goal was increased in 1980 to 85.4 million pounds; new purchases in 1981 brought stockpile supplies to 46 million pounds. The U.S. imported 91 percent of its cobalt requirements in 1981.

COLUMBIUM (Cb)

Columbium is a shiny soft white metal similar to copper in weight and hardness. The addition of small amounts of columbium to plain carbon steel improves the steel's hardness and strength; the addition of larger amounts of columbium yields steels useful for oil and gas pipelines, for structural shapes and for parts in cars and trucks. Still higher proportions of columbium are used to make superalloys for blades and vanes in jet turbines, rocket subassemblies and heat-resistant combustion equipment. At extremely low temperatures, columbium becomes a superconductor, offering virtually zero resistance to the passage of an electric current. The metal is also called niobium, its scientific name, but the term *columbium* is more commonly used in the metallurgical industry.

Brazil is by far the world's most important source of columbium, accounting for some 80 percent of the non-Communist world's production and 57 percent of its known reserves. Canada, Thailand, Malaysia and Nigeria are also producers of columbium.

Because relatively small quantities of columbium are required for metallurgical use, total production in the non-Communist world is only about 24.5 million pounds a year. U.S. consumption is expected to rise at an annual rate of 6 percent through 1990.

World supplies of columbium, mainly from Brazil, have kept pace with demand, and the market price has risen only a little more swiftly than world inflation, from $1.65 a pound for contained metal in 1970 to $6.12 a pound in 1982.

Stockpile position and import dependence: During the 1960s and early 1970s the U.S. government sold excess columbium from its stockpile inventories. In 1980 the stockpile goal was raised to 4.85 million pounds, mainly in the form of columbium concentrates. In 1981 the inventory was 2,510,528 pounds of contained metal. With no domestic production of columbium, the U.S. is 100 percent dependent upon imports.

COPPER (Cu)

Copper is a metal of reddish brown color, an excellent conductor of heat and electricity, and a material so easy to recover from its ores that primitive tribes made tools, weapons and ornaments of copper. To modern man, copper is synonymous with the electrical industry, serving in generators, motors and power transmission systems. The metal is also used in roofing, plumbing, household utensils, jewelry and coinage.

The U.S. has been a leading copper-producing country since 1883; in 1980 it was followed in order by Chile, the USSR, Canada, Zaire and Zambia. But even with its large production, the U.S. was a net importer of copper, principally from Canada, Chile, Zambia and Peru.

Copper smelters, which emit sulfur compounds, trace elements and particulates, have been affected by air pollution control regulations. The Bureau of Mines reports that production at some smelters has been curtailed and construction of new facilities delayed because of problems in meeting air quality standards at economic cost. Some industry spokesmen believe that strict enforcement of air quality standards may lead to the closing of other smelters and a growing U.S. dependence upon imported copper.

In the U.S., about 99 percent of mine production comes from ores recovered primarily for their copper content. Copper ores are also the source of the country's entire production of arsenic, rhenium, selenium, tellurium, platinum and palladium, as well as significant amounts of gold, silver, molybdenum, nickel, uranium, iron, lead, zinc and sulfur. The copper mines of Zaire are also the source of much of the world's cobalt.

In the decade of the 1970s the price of copper rose at a slower rate than inflation, from 58¢ a pound in 1970 to $1.10 in 1980. The 1981–82 recession forced the price of copper down to 55¢ in mid-1982.

Stockpile position and import dependence: In March 1981 the stockpile goal for copper was one million tons; previously held supplies had been sold and there was no copper in inventory. In 1981 the U.S. imported 5 percent of its net consumption.

GALLIUM (Ga)

Gallium in its pure state is a silvery white metal, first isolated by a French chemist in 1875 and named in honor of France (Gallia in Latin). The metal occurs in low concentration in ores of zinc and aluminum, but until its peculiar electronic properties were discovered there was little incentive to recover and process it. Now it could well emerge as one of the wonder metals of the future.

Gallium compounds are used in light-emitting diodes, the illuminating elements in the dials of electronic instruments, in light detectors and other photoelectric applications. Gallium semiconductor compounds are used in the manufacture of calculators, radios, television and high-fidelity sound equipment, and in fiber optics, the new technology that is revolutionizing the transmission of television and voice communications.

Some experts believe that gallium will displace silicon in some electronic devices, and that it will come into wider use in photovoltaic cells, to generate electricity from sunlight. While silicon, the more commonly used element in such cells, can convert about 17 percent of the potential energy from sunlight into electricity, gallium's theoretical efficiency is around 25 percent. Any large increase in demand for photovoltaic cells could increase the demand for gallium.

Although there are plentiful amounts of gallium in base metal ores found in the U.S., the high cost of chemically separating gallium keeps the cost of the metal and its compounds high. In fact, much of the U.S. supply in recent years has been imported from Switzerland and West Germany. Total gallium production in the U.S. in 1981 was estimated at 4,800 kilograms, against a consumption of 8,000 kilograms. Major funding of aerospace and other research and development programs may increase the demand for gallium, and may also lead to expansion of U.S. production.

Although the production and consumption of gallium remain quite small, the price of gallium has actually declined within the past decade, from $700 a kilo in 1970 to $350 a kilo in 1982.

Stockpile position and import dependence: Gallium is not held in the U.S. strategic stockpile and there is no goal for accumulation. Import dependence in 1980 was 70 percent.

GERMANIUM (Ge)

Germanium, an elusive element undiscovered until 1886, is a grayish white substance, lustrous, hard, brittle, displaying some but not all of the properties of a metal and is thus defined as a metalloid. It is recovered from the residues of zinc ores.

The peculiar properties of germanium began to be appreciated after the invention of the transistor in 1947 inaugurated the age of the semiconductor. Germanium is used in the manufacture of transistors, diodes and rectifiers; more recently it has come into demand for use in lasers, infrared optics and fiber optic technology. It has many applications in weaponry, in guidance systems for missiles and in night sights for fire control systems, among other uses.

Before the mid-1970s the major world source of germanium was the giant Tsumeb base metal mine in South West Africa; with the exhaustion of the principal germanium-bearing ores there, production shifted to the processing of zinc ores elsewhere in the world, including the U.S. There is no real shortage of germanium-bearing ores, but the extraction of germanium as a trace element is difficult and costly, and tends to sustain the price of the element and its compounds. Producer prices have varied from $280 a kilogram in 1970 to as high as $834 in 1980. Dealer prices have ranged as high as $1,000 a kilogram; in mid-1982 the price was $800 a kilogram. Demand for germanium is expected to rise at an annual rate of 4 to 5 percent through the 1990s. U.S. consumption was estimated at 38,000 kilograms for 1981.

Stockpile position and import dependence: While germanium is potentially a critical material because of its defense applications, a 1977 government study concluded that domestic production potential made stockpiling unnecessary. There is no stockpile goal or inventory in germanium. Import dependence is about 23 percent.

INDIUM (In)

Indium is a soft silver-white metal found as a trace constituent most commonly in association with zinc, but also with lead, tin, tungsten and iron minerals. It is used in solders and sealers, as an alloy with precious and base metals and in high-purity state in preformed shapes in electronic components. Compounds of indium are used in the manufacture of light-emitting diodes for watch dials and electronic instruments.

A number of laboratories have been investigating the use of indium in solar cells for the generation of electricity from sunlight. If successful, this research could lead to much broader commercial use of indium.

World production of indium is largely dependent upon the rate of zinc production. The chief exporters of indium to the U.S. are Peru, Belgium-Luxembourg, the United Kingdom and Canada. U.S. consumption, in the range of 650,000 troy ounces a year, accounts for about 30 percent of all the world's use of the metal, and is expected to increase by 3 percent a year through 1990.

The producer price of indium has risen from $2.50 a troy ounce in 1970 to $14.50 an ounce in 1980; dealer sales in the range of $20 an ounce were reported in 1981. Prices were lower and erratic in 1982 and fell as low as $2.90 an ounce.

Stockpile position and import dependence: Indium is not held in the strategic stockpile. U.S. import dependence is not reported by the Bureau of Mines, but is believed to exceed 50 percent.

LEAD (Pb)

Lead is a heavy soft metal long known and used by man. The hanging gardens of Babylon were floored with soldered sheets of lead. Some early winemakers sold their product in earthenware vessels glazed with lead, and may have slowly poisoned some of their customers before coming to understand the toxic properties of lead and the importance of proper firing techniques in pottery making.

The largest modern-day use of lead is in lead-acid storage batteries, widely employed in the automotive industry and in many other applications. Large quantities of lead were formerly used as an antiknock additive in gasoline for high-compression engines, but air quality regulations are limiting their use. Lead is used to sheathe electrical cables and as an ingredient in industrial paints, and it is the most efficient of the common metals as a shield against radiation. Lead is often alloyed with antimony as a hardening agent, and with calcium, tin, selenium, cadmium and copper for special applications.

While newer technologies may eventually supplant lead in storage batteries, the conventional lead-acid battery is expected to survive in many uses for the next 15 to 20 years. Although lead is no longer used for interior paints because of its toxicity, lead paints are still widely used in construction, particularly where anticorrosion and waterproofing qualities are required. The Bureau of Mines expects that overall demand for lead will rise by 1.2 percent a year to the end of this century.

The price of lead rose from 15.7¢ a pound in 1970 to 52.6¢ in 1979, falling to 42.4¢ in 1980 and to the range of 22.5¢ a pound in 1982. This recession in metal prices was one of the factors in a decision by the Bunker Hill Co. to retire its aging lead smelter in Kellogg, Idaho, early in 1982. The closure of that plant leaves five active lead smelters in the U.S.

Stockpile position and import dependence: The government has bought and sold lead for the stockpile in recent years. In March

1981 the stockpile goal was 1,100,000 short tons and the inventory 601,036 tons. While the U.S. is normally a small net importer of lead (10 percent in 1981) it was a small net exporter in 1980.

LITHIUM (Li)

Lithium, the lightest of the metals, is soft and ductile and highly reactive to water. In its metallic form it burns spontaneously at 175° C.; its most common forms are as lithium carbonate and lithium hydroxide.

The largest end use of lithium is in aluminum potlines, accounting for about one-third of domestic consumption. It is also a component of lubricating compounds, and is used in the manufacture of ceramics and in glass. The use of a lithium ion together with a silver halide causes clear glass to turn dark on exposure to sunlight, the principle employed in instant sunglasses.

Nonrechargeable batteries using lithium metal have long life and high reliability, making them especially useful in such applications as heart pacemakers, cameras, calculators and hearing aids. Lithium's light weight and its electrolytic qualites have led to a great deal of research on the development of durable lightweight batteries that could bring battery-powered automobiles into the realm of the practical. Investigations are also under way to develop lithium batteries that could be charged in periods of lower power demand and used to meet part of the peak demand in electric utilities. Successful development of either of these applications could vastly increase the world demand for lithium.

The U.S. produces all the lithium it needs and an exportable surplus, much of it from underground mines in Nevada, most of the rest from solid ores in North Carolina. Lithium reserves in Chile are larger than those of the U.S., which is the world's leading producer.

The price of lithium metal has risen gradually from $9 a pound in 1970 to $19 a pound in 1982.

Stockpile position and import dependence: Lithium is not held in the strategic stockpile. The U.S. is a net exporter.

MANGANESE (Mn)

Manganese, an unglamorous black rock when it is dug from the ground, a gray-white brittle solid in its metallic state, is one of the industrial world's most basic raw materials. Used to remove oxygen and sulfur from molten steel and to harden and toughen the final product, it is essential to the manufacture of most steels and important in the production of cast iron, aluminum and dry-cell batteries.

Brazil, long a supplier of manganese to the U.S., is nearing the exhaustion of its best mines and it plans to reserve much of its future production for its own steel industry. Gabon is the largest supplier of manganese ore to the U.S., and South Africa is the leading supplier of the more highly processed ferromanganese.

Trade patterns in manganese have shifted. In earlier years most manganese used by American steelmakers was imported as ore and processed with American coal and labor into ferromanganese. Now South Africa has developed its own ferromanganese industry using its cheap coal to turn out a product more economical for American companies than U.S.-made ferromanganese. This economic streamlining, however, has led to the shrinkage of American smelting capacity for ferromanganese, leaving the country more vulnerable to supply interruptions and less capable of processing the ores held in the strategic stockpile.

The price of manganese was 50¢ a pound of electrolytic metal in 1970. The price rose to 68¢ in 1980 and sank to 50¢ in mid-1982. The mining of manganese, especially from South Africa's rich surface deposits, is relatively simple, and much of the cost is represented by transportation and processing costs. U.S. consumption is expected to rise by 1.4 percent a year to the end of this century.

While enormous reserves of manganese are known to exist on the floor of the Pacific, Atlantic and Indian oceans, the recovery of these resources is not likely to become a market factor before the 1990s.

Stockpile position and import dependence: The revised stockpile goal is 1.5 million tons of contained metal in ores of several grades; the inventory is 1,586,353 tons of contained metal in stockpile-grade ore. Import dependence of the U.S. was 98 percent in 1981.

MOLYBDENUM (Mo)

Molybdenum is a silver-white metallic element used principally as an alloying agent in the production of steel, to add toughness, hardness and strength. Chemical and other nonmetallurgical uses account for about 10 percent of consumption.

Molybdenum-bearing armor plate was first produced in France in

1894. World War I increased the demand for molybdenum for steels in various forms of armament, and most steels used for military purposes still depend upon molybdenum for strength and toughness.

Molybdenum steels are particularly useful in the manufacture of tubing, for boilers, heat exchangers, distillation and refining machinery and for pipelines, especially those in which extremes of cold may be encountered. Most industrial steels contain some molybdenum. The pure metal, molybdenum, has some applications in highly technical industries such as nuclear energy, aerospace and electronics.

Most of the world's reserves of molybdenum occur in the western mountains of North and South America; the U.S. has 53 percent of the world molybdenum reserves and in 1980 accounted for 61 percent of world production. Colorado and New Mexico are the major producing states for molybdenum ore, while mines in Arizona, California, New Mexico and Utah produce molybdenum as a coproduct with other metals. U.S. demand is expected to grow by 4.2 percent a year through 1990.

The price of molybdenum rose from $1.92 a pound in 1970 to as high as $9.70 a pound in 1980 and 1981, but fell under reduced recessionary demand to $4.50 a pound in 1982.

Stockpile position and import dependence: The strategic stockpile has no goal or inventory in molybdenum. The U.S. is a substantial net exporter.

NICKEL (Ni)

Nickel is a light gray, tough, ductile metal used mainly in the manufacture of high-strength, corrosion-resistant steels, and in combination with copper, chromium and cobalt to form alloys resistant to corrosion from chemicals and salt water. Nickel is also a component of the superalloys developed since World War II for use in jet aircraft engines.

The only significant nickel-mining operation in the U.S is an open-pit mine at Riddle, Oregon. A nickel-copper refinery at Port Nickel, Louisiana, operated by Amax Inc., processes ore from African sources; it produced about 32,500 tons of nickel in 1979. Canada is the leading world producer of nickel, providing the U.S. with a reasonably secure source of supply for this highly strategic metal.

Environmental considerations are a growing factor in the production of nickel. In 1980 the government of Canada placed a limit on sulfur dioxide emissions from a large nickel smelter in Sudbury, Ontario, effectively limiting the smelter's production to 280 million pounds of nickel a year. In the U.S. a nickel-copper mining project under development in Minnesota was canceled because of changes in state environmental regulations.

The development of seabed mining could greatly expand world production of nickel, but efforts by Canada to limit nickel production from this source, and negotiating strategies by Third World countries at the United Nations Conference on Law of the Sea, have served to postpone the time when the seabed can be successfully exploited for minerals.

The price of nickel rose from $1.28 a pound in 1970 to around $3.50 a pound in 1981, dropping to $2.37 in mid-1982.

Stockpile position and import dependence: The strategic stockpile has a goal of 200,000 tons of nickel, but none in inventory as of late 1981. U.S. import dependence was 72 percent of consumption in 1981.

PLATINUM GROUP METALS

The platinum group metals are six closely related elements commonly occurring together in nature and sharing physical and chemical characteristics. The metals are platinum (Pt), palladium (Pd), rhodium (Rh), ruthenium (Ru), iridium (Ir) and osmium (Os). All of the platinum group metals retain their shape and strength under high temperatures; several of them are extremely useful in industry because of their resistance to corrosion and their ability to catalyze chemical reactions among other elements.

South Africa is the leading producer of platinum metals, followed by the Soviet Union and more distantly by Canada. In South Africa, a number of mines are operated primarily for their platinum values, with copper, cobalt, gold and nickel as by-products. In the Soviet Union and Canada, platinum is a by-product of other minerals, usually nickel or copper.

In recent years in the U.S., the automobile industry has been by far the biggest consumer of platinum group metals, principally in catalytic converters to reduce objectionable exhaust emissions. A typical converter uses about .05 troy ounce of a platinum-palladium alloy; the use of rhodium for this purpose is increasing.

In the chemical industry, the platinum metals are employed in a wide variety of processes, including the manufacture of nitric acid, one step in the production of nitrogen-based fertilizers. In petroleum refining, catalysts of platinum, platinum-iridium and platinum-rhenium are used in a process to upgrade the octane rating of gasoline. The platinum metals have many other applications in electronic and electrical equipment, in the manufacture of glass and glass fiber and synthetic fibers.

Ruthenium and osmium have fewer practical applications than other members of the platinum group, and their prices declined from 1970 to 1980, ruthenium from $55 to $45 a troy ounce, osmium from $215 to $150. The other metals of the group have all risen in price in the same period: platinum from $133 to $420 an ounce; palladium from $38 to $225; rhodium from $358 to $800; iridium from $260 to $500. Dealer or free-market prices fluctuated far more than producer prices, and in mid-1982 were in the range of $250 for platinum, $51 for palladium, $320 for rhodium, $360 for iridium, $130 for osmium and $25 for ruthenium.

Stockpile position and import dependence: Three of the platinum group metals are held in the strategic stockpile. In 1981 the stockpile positions were:

	Goal	Inventory
Platinum	1,310,000 ounces	453,000 ounces
Palladium	3,000,000	1,255,000
Iridium	98,000	17,000

The U.S. produces 1 percent of its platinum needs as a by-product of copper mining, meets another 12 percent by recycling and is 87 percent dependent upon imports.

RHENIUM (Re)

Rhenium, a rare metallic element, remained undiscovered until 1925, when three German scientists proved its existence and named it for the Rhine river. Before World War II it was produced only from copper-smelter residues in Germany; since the 1940s it has also been produced from flue dusts and gases generated in the roasting of copper-molybdenite ores. Chile has emerged as the leading world producer of the metal.

Rhenium's principal use has been in platinum-rhenium catalysts for the production of low-lead and lead-free high-octane gasoline. Smaller amounts of the metal are used in thermocouples, heating elements, temperature controls and X-ray equipment. Research continues on the development of new high-temperature alloys containing rhenium for use in jet engine turbine blades; further uses are anticipated in semiconductors, resistors, small electromagnets and other catalytic applications.

Total world production of rhenium for 1980 was estimated at 17,500 pounds, so rapid fluctuation in its price is not surprising. The price pattern has reflected large changes in both production and demand; from $1,000 a pound in 1970 the price dropped to $350 a pound in 1978. Then a sharp increase in demand for the manufacture of lead-free gasoline elevated the price of rhenium to as high as $2,500 a pound in 1980. In mid-1982 the metal was marketed at around $550 a pound.

Stockpile position and import dependence: Rhenium is not stockpiled. The U.S. imports 60 percent of its rhenium requirements, mostly from Chile and West Germany.

SELENIUM (Se)

Selenium is a nonmetallic element chemically resembling sulfur and tellurium; it is commonly recovered as a by-product of the electrolytic refining of copper. Its commercial importance lies in its uses in electronic components, in photoelectric devices and in photographic copying applications, where its unique quality is its ability to transfer a photographic image by means of static electricity.

The oldest use of selenium is in glass manufacturing, to neutralize the green tint caused by iron compounds. It is added to stainless steels to improve casting, forging and machining characteristics without reducing corrosion resistance.

Selenium has been in oversupply in the U.S. in recent years, and its price has reflected this soft market. The producer price of selenium stood at $9 a pound in 1970, rose to $18 a pound in the mid-1970s, and by 1982 had fallen to $3.50 a pound.

Stockpile position and import dependence: All selenium stocks held in the national stockpile were sold in the early 1970s, and the stockpile quota was reduced to zero. Import dependence was 49 percent in 1981.

SILVER (Ag)

Silver, one of the precious or "noble" metals, is also a highly versatile industrial raw material, an important defense-related metal and the object of worldwide market speculation. Physical silver is bought and sold through the London Metal Exchange, and futures contracts are traded on exchanges in New York and Chicago. Anyone with an investment in silver can follow its price variations at almost any hour of the day or night.

An oddity of the silver market is that world consumption for industrial uses and coinage regularly exceeds world mine production by a wide margin. This deficit is filled by melting of ingots, coins and other silver objects. Much of the metal appears from India, where the hoarding of silver has been a folk custom for centuries. Excluding Communist-dominated areas, world consumption of silver in 1980 exceeded mine production by some 40 percent, or 100 million ounces.

In the U.S., major uses of silver are in photography, sterlingware and electrical contacts and batteries; smaller amounts are used for jewelry, dental and medical purposes and for medallions and commemorative objects. The U.S. Bureau of Mines estimates that demand for silver in the U.S. will increase at a rate of 3.1 percent from 1978 to the end of the century.

The price of silver has fluctuated wildly in recent years, from an average of $1.77 an ounce in 1977, down to $1.55 an ounce in 1971, and rising on average through the rest of the decade to enter 1980 on a burst of worldwide speculative demand that pushed the price briefly to almost $50 an ounce before breaking sharply. Silver traded in the range of $8 to $12 an ounce during much of 1981 and fell to $5 to $6 an ounce in mid-1982.

Stockpile position and import dependence: Because of its many uses in defense industries, silver has long been held in the strategic stockpile. The stockpile inventory stood at 139.5 million ounces in 1981 when Congress authorized a series of auctions designed to sell off 105 million ounces over a three-year period to raise funds for purchase of other critical and strategic materials. While the U.S. has usually been an importer of silver in recent years, import dependence has fluctuated from 7 percent in 1980 to 50 percent in 1981.

TANTALUM (Ta)

Tantalum is a very hard, dense metal, stable at high temperatures, resistant to corrosion, and in demand for such strategic applications as aircraft, missiles, radio communications, machine tools and nuclear devices. World demand increased sharply during the last decade to just over two million pounds a year.

Tantalum is often found in combination with columbium; Canada, Brazil, Australia, Nigeria and Mozambique are among the significant producers of the ore. In addition, Thailand and Malaysia have produced substantial amounts of the metal by reprocessing slags from tin smelters. The Bureau of Mines observes in *Mineral Facts and Problems,* 1980 edition: "The reliability of some important foreign sources is subject to political and social factors that could reduce the U.S. supply of tantalum, thereby causing short-term shortages." The Soviet Union is presumed to be self-sufficient in tantalum, but has assigned a group of experts to try to improve production in mines in Mozambique.

The electronics industry absorbs two-thirds of the tantalum used in the U.S.; the tantalum capacitor has become the standard for reliable performance. For the metalworking industry tantalum carbide makes excellent cutting, boring and drilling tools. About 8 percent of total consumption of tantalum goes into the aerospace industry, for jet engines and gas turbine parts. Use of tantalum is expected to rise by about 4.1 percent a year to the end of the century.

The producer price of tantalum has reflected a growing demand and the political instability of some key producing areas. From $9.15 a pound in 1970, the price moved up to $115 in 1981 and sank to $37 a pound in 1982.

Stockpile position and import dependence: The stockpile goal for tantalum was increased in 1980 to 7.2 million pounds; inventory in 1981 was 2.4 million pounds. There is no mine production of tantalum in the U.S. With some recycling of used metal, import dependence in 1981 was rated at 91 percent.

TIN (Sn)

Tin is a soft silver-colored metal, malleable, with a low melting point. It was one of the first metals known to man, and bronze, an alloy of tin and copper, gave its name to an age in which man first

developed metallic tools for hunting and war. Tin is still a war material, used in engine bearings, solders and electrical gear, but one of
its largest uses is for plating steel to make "tin" containers.

Because reserves of tin ore in the U.S. are extremely small, tin
has long been one of the most critical of the strategic metals. Before
World War II, most of America's tin came from Southeast Asia and
from Bolivian ore that was first shipped to Europe for smelting. As
war approached in 1941, the U.S. set up a tin smelter in Texas City,
Texas, capable of processing the low-grade ores from Bolivia. At the
same time, the government stepped up its imports from Southeast
Asia while the trade routes were still open. With the stockpile thus
constructed, with production from the Texas smelter and by rigor-
ous conservation, the U.S. met its military needs in World War II.

In recent years, the principal tin-producing countries have been
Malaysia, with close to 29 percent of world production, Thailand,
Indonesia, the Soviet Union, China and Bolivia. Several of the tin-
producing countries have built smelters in order to export metal
rather than ore and concentrates. The U.S. consumes about one-
fourth of the world's output of tin.

The price of tin rose from $1.74 a pound in 1970 to $8.46 in 1980.
In 1981 the price was around $8.05 in the open market; under
weight of a worldwide recession it sank to $4.28 in mid-1982.

Stockpile position and import dependence: Over the years to
1980, the government stockpile inventory in tin rose to 203,691
tons, far above the goal, which was revised upward that year to
42,000 tons. Some small sales were made from the stockpile, and on
March 31, 1981, the inventory was down to 200,112 tons. Import
dependence was 80 percent in 1981.

TITANIUM (Ti)

Titanium is a silvery white metal of unique value in aircraft and
missiles because of its great strength and light weight. In terms of
tonnages of contained metal, 92 percent of the titanium consumed in
the U.S. is used for pigments in paints, paper and plastics and for
other chemical products, but titanium derives its strategic importance from the 8 percent of consumption used as metal. About 60
percent of the titanium metal consumed in the U.S. goes into parts
and assemblies for civilian and military aircraft, jet engines, guided
missiles and spacecraft. The remainder is used in chemical and elec-

trochemical industries, in marine applications, military ordnance and for other purposes.

The major titanium-bearing minerals are ilmenite and rutile. The former is more common and is the usual source for titanium for pigments; rutile is rarer, and the major raw material for making sponge metal. While the U.S. has concentrations of ilmenite in Florida, New York and New Jersey, its resources in rutile are mostly subeconomic, and the nation depends upon imports of rutile and titanium sponge, much of it from Australian sources.

As late as 1976–79, the USSR supplied 21 percent of the titanium sponge used in the U.S., but in 1979 and later it greatly reduced its sales and began purchasing ore and metal in world markets. Since more than 65 percent of Soviet consumption of titanium is believed to be for weaponry, this suggested that an arms buildup and stock-piling program was in progress, and that in the future the Soviet Union will be more of a competitor than a supplier to the West for titanium. The Soviet Union is believed to be building deep-diving, high-speed nuclear-powered submarines with hulls of titanium.

From 1970 to 1980, the price of rutile pigment increased from 45¢ to 98¢ a pound, but the more strategically important sponge metal rose in price from $1.32 to $7.02 a pound in producer contracts. In 1982, the free-market (dealer) price fell to about $2.50 a pound.

Stockpile position and import dependence: The stockpile goal for titanium sponge is 195,000 short tons; in 1981 the inventory stood at 32,331 tons and a purchase program for the stockpile was planned but not funded. Three American producers of sponge increased their capacity during the year. U.S. import dependence was esti-mated at 18 percent of consumption.

TUNGSTEN (W)

Tungsten, a silvery gray metal, is one of the heaviest of the ele-ments, and has the highest melting point of any metal, 3,410° C. The extreme hardness of tungsten carbide at high working tempera-tures makes it a preferred material for the cutting edges of machine tools; it is used extensively in drill bits, in the cutting edges of earth-moving equipment and in crushing machinery. Tungsten is used in a wide variety of superalloys where strength at high temperatures is demanded, and as the core material for armor-piercing projectiles. Depleted uranium is also used for this purpose.

The U.S. has significant resources and production of tungsten, mainly from mines in California, Colorado and Nevada; it also imports concentrates from Canada, Bolivia (where tungsten is a co-product with tin), Thailand and China. In the 1950s, when imports of tungsten from China were cut off because of the Korean War, the U.S. employed the Defense Production Act to stimulate domestic mining, and the General Services Administration built up large stockpile reserves. After the major stockpile purchases were completed in 1959, a number of U.S. mines were closed; some remain as potential sources for future needs.

The Bureau of Mines estimates U.S. requirements in tungsten will increase by 4.5 percent a year through 1990. For the world as a whole, demand is projected to grow at a rate of 3.2 percent a year from 1978 to the year 2000.

Tungsten was marketed under producer contracts at $2.55 a pound in 1970, at $8.27 a pound in 1979. In 1982, the free-market price was in the neighborhood of $5 a pound.

Stockpile position and import dependence: The stockpile goal is 50,666,000 pounds of contained tungsten. The inventory was 81.8 million pounds in 1980 and sales were authorized to reduce the inventory and provide funds for the purchase of other materials. In 1980 import dependence was 54 percent.

VANADIUM (V)

Vanadium is a gray to white metal that can be beaten into shapes or drawn into wire. It is usually found in ores in combination with other metals such as uranium or iron, though in the U.S., one deposit, near Hot Springs, Arkansas, is mined for its vanadium content. Vanadium's major use is as an alloy in the manufacture of iron and steel. It is also used to alloy titanium, and as a chemical catalyst in making sulfuric acid.

The U.S. is the world's largest consumer of vanadium; with deposits in the Rocky Mountains as well as in Arkansas, it is the third-ranking producer, following South Africa and the USSR. The USSR is believed to be about self-sufficient in the metal. South Africa is a substantial exporter.

Steel alloyed with vanadium resists abrasion and so is used to make high-speed tools. Other vanadium steels are used in high-speed machine parts, in strength-demanding applications such as gears and crankshafts, and in heavy-duty equipment and machinery.

In relatively good supply, vanadium has experienced only a moderate price increase in recent years, advancing from $4.37 a pound in 1970 to $6.34 in 1980. In mid-1982 the dealer price was $6.09 a pound.

Stockpile position and import dependence: The stockpile goal is 8,700 short tons of vanadium and the inventory 541 tons. U.S. import dependence in 1981 was 42 percent.

ZINC (Zn)

Zinc is a bluish white metal, chemically active and widely used to protect iron and steel products against corrosion and as a component along with copper in the manufacture of brass. Zinc was known and used in the pre-Christian era by the Chinese, Indians and Romans.

From 1901 through 1971 the U.S. was the world's largest producer of zinc, but in the last decade it became increasingly dependent upon imports as nearly a dozen smelters closed for economic reasons, including the cost of meeting strict environmental standards. A number of metals are recovered largely as a by-product of zinc smelting, and a decline in zinc-smelting capacity may affect the supply of cadmium, germanium, thallium, indium and gallium.

Although the zinc market suffered in 1980 and 1981 because of a recession in the automobile and housing industries, the Bureau of Mines forecasts that demand will rise at a rate of 1.8 percent a year to the end of the century. Zinc is used in galvanizing, in brass and bronze products, in automobile parts and batteries, and in many construction materials and in construction equipment. Chemical compounds of zinc are widely used in rubber manufacturing and in other chemical industries.

The price of zinc has moved from 15¢ a pound in 1970 to 37.5¢ in 1980. Dealer prices fell to around 29¢ in 1982.

Stockpile position and import dependence: The strategic stockpile has a goal of 1,425,000 short tons in 1981 and an inventory of 375,970 tons. U.S. import dependence was 67 percent in 1981.

ZIRCONIUM (Zr) AND HAFNIUM (Hf)

Zirconium and hafnium, both gray metallic elements, are found in the same mineral, zircon, in the ratio of 50 to 1. In their metallic forms, both elements are widely used in nuclear engineering.

Zirconium sands are used in foundries, and in the manufacture of ceramics and abrasives. Zircon metal with its superb resistance to corrosion under extreme heat and radiation is used for the cladding of fuel rods and in structural materials in nuclear reactors and in chemical-processing equipment.

More than 85 percent of all hafnium produced is consumed in the form of metal, and much of that for control rods in the nuclear reactors of U.S. naval vessels. It is a preferred material where relatively maintenance-free operation is necessary.

The sands from which the two metals are recovered are found in Tennessee, New Jersey, South Carolina and California. Australia is the major foreign source of zircon sands, and South Africa also is known to have extensive reserves.

The producer price of zirconium was around $6 a pound in 1970 and rose to $17 a pound in 1981. In mid-1982 producers were offering it for sale at $9.50 to $15 a pound, depending upon the quantity ordered. The price of hafnium ranged from $85 a pound in 1970 to as high as $125 in 1981. In mid-1982 dealers were offering it at $84 a pound in larger amounts, $105 a pound for small orders.

Stockpile position and import dependence: Neither zirconium nor hafnium is held in the federal strategic stockpile, although the Department of Defense at year-end 1979 held approximately 1,152 tons of zirconium metal and 32 tons of hafnium in inventory. In 1981 the U.S. imported an estimated 62 percent of the ore from which both metals are recovered.

10

The Case for Strategic Investments

For reasons explained in the preceding chapters, the prospect appears likely that in the years ahead the world will face shortages in some of the most vital raw materials. This risk threatens to cause a seismic shift in world power patterns. The industrial nations will have to give a higher priority than in the past to securing sources of key materials and protecting the sea-lanes by which these commodities move to market. Producers and exporters of strategic metals will enjoy an unmatched opportunity to use their resources as geopolitical levers. Whether they will possess the political and diplomatic skills to profit from their opportunity without being drawn into the new Communist colonial empire is still an open question.

The coming world scarcity will also present opportunities for cool-headed investors capable of weighing risks, avoiding pitfalls and moving decisively into favorable situations. Lacking a crystal ball, we cannot tell you where and when the most promising opportunities will emerge. But in this and the following chapters, we will try to provide you with a kind of mariner's chart to the brightest prospects for a profit, and also warn of the rocks and shoals that threaten the unwary.

At the heart of the problem lies the Soviet Union, rich in oil and other strategic minerals, its industries backward and inefficient, its agriculture chaotic and vulnerable to the vagaries of a brutal climate. To generate funds for its essential imports, the Soviet Union sells oil, gold and a variety of solid minerals, but it conceals its purposes behind a security curtain, and rarely moves in the direction that simple commercial considerations would suggest. Strategic rather than economic goals appear to dominate its behavior, and thus for reasons often unclear to the West, Moscow sells or withholds its strategic minerals in unpredictable patterns. The Soviet Union is not a reliable trading partner, and the West has been forced to develop alternate sources, even for minerals that the Soviets are believed to produce in abundance.

In the long reach of history, access to raw materials and trading routes ("freedom of the seas") has been a classic root cause of conflict among nations, and in the ongoing rivalry between East and West this pattern could play itself out again. Shortages of food and limited economic development in the Soviet Union or the Third World, or denial of essential resources to the West, could surely create international tensions capable of slipping out of control.

It is a normal role of private investors and their professional advisors to try to anticipate geopolitical trends and to act upon their interpretation of events. In a world where lack of manganese could shut down whole steel industries, where lack of cobalt could silence a nation's jet fleets and lack of platinum severely impair chemical and refining industries, the potential for international conflict over control of key resources cannot be dismissed.

THE MARKETS

While sources, supply routes and price patterns are well established for the major industrial metals, the changing technology of modern industry is constantly affecting the markets for the more obscure "minor metals," which may gain considerable importance even though their total world production is only a few thousand kilograms a year. New developments in solar power generation, electronics, oil refining and weapons technology have created sharp increases in demand and price for such metals as gallium, germanium, indium and rhenium. Total world production of these metals in 1981 as estimated by the U.S. Bureau of Mines are: gallium, 12,000 to 20,000 kilograms; germanium, 125,000 kilograms; indium, about 44,000 kilograms; rhenium, 27,500 pounds. In these metals, the alert investor is better situated than an inertia-ridden government agency to respond to changing markets and prices.

As trading practices develop and mature, the efficiency and liquidity of markets increases. New market operators enter the field. Information becomes more available and more accessible. The Reuters Money Wire system offers its subscribers up-to-the-minute market information on a wide range of "minor metals," accessible on a cathode-ray tube upon keying the proper codes. Fifteen to 20 of the commonly traded metals are tracked by Reuters.

A growing interest in the investment potential of strategic metals has led a number of nationally known brokerage firms to offer specialized services in the buying and selling of these commodities.

When E. F. Hutton speaks about strategic metals, more and more people are listening. Bache & Co., another nationally known brokerage firm with a renowned commodites trading department, has also moved into the field. The New York-based Sinclair Group Companies (headed by one of the authors of this book) has created a subsidiary known as Strategic Metals and Critical Materials Inc. to trade in minor metals for its own account and to provide brokerage services for its clients.

The state of the markets in critical and strategic materials in 1982 might be compared with the state of the markets in over-the-counter securities before the development of automated quote systems for market-making in NASDAQ-listed stocks and inactively traded securities. Public markets for critical and strategic materials are expanding as supply, industrial demand and trading volume increase; these new markets enhance an investor's ability to enter the market with the assurance of being able to buy and sell at prices reasonably reflecting current conditions in an efficient market.

CAVEAT EMPTOR, OR DO YOU KNOW WHO YOUR BROKER IS?

Along with a number of thoroughly reputable and well-financed investment firms, the new field of strategic-metals trading has attracted a quota of unscrupulous operators, more intent on turning a quick profit for themselves than in educating their customer or building a long-term business relationship with him or her. State and federal securities regulators have been alerted to some of the sharp practices and shady operators entering the field and are taking appropriate action to protect the public. But to paraphrase the slogan of a well-known discount clothier, an educated consumer is the best customer, in strategic metals as in many other areas. The investor's best protection lies in his own understanding of the field, and in being alert to the possible pitfalls.

An investor should understand that no broker can legitimately "guarantee" a profit to the buyer, and any smooth-talking telephone caller offering a sure thing should be heard with the utmost skepticism. Second, the investor should be aware that except for the precious metals platinum, silver and copper, none the strategic metals is traded in the U.S. in the form of futures contracts. The investor should expect to buy and fully pay for any materials he acquires.

Other traps for the unwary are the offering of metals at unrealistically high prices in terms of the market, or materials not of commercial grade and therefore difficult to resell. A few tenths of 1 percent in the purity of cobalt and some other metals will make a substantial difference in the market value of the product, so the offering of low-grade material at high-grade prices is, unfortunately, one of the pitfalls to watch for. Beyond that, any salesman exerting undue pressure to "buy now before the price goes up" may be trying to coerce his customer into acting with insufficient information. Use of any of these high-pressure tactics, especially by a telephone caller whom you have never heard of, should serve as a red flag of warning.

MARKET TIMING

It is an axiom in investing that the time to buy is when buyers are scarce, and the time to sell is when others are clamoring to buy. This basic truth is as valid in strategic investment as in any others.

The early 1980s has been a period of worldwide industrial recession and the prices of many industrial materials including strategic metals have fallen below their long-term trend lines. This has been true for cobalt, chromium, manganese, platinum and many other metals. This suggests that a long-term buying opportunity prevails for investors willing to apply their intelligence and commit their funds to a form of investment still unfamiliar to many. This favorable period for investment may not last beyond early 1983. The time to sell will arrive when tensions rise, materials shortages develop or threaten, and buyers actively bid for available supplies of commodities that the prudent and farsighted have purchased and stored earlier.

An investor who takes into account long-term market cycles, who follows and interprets geopolitical developments, who enters the market with professional care and exits under the guidance of intelligence rather than emotion, may enjoy substantial long-term profits for his foresight. He may also help his country to weather the materials crises that almost surely lie ahead.

THE PRIVATE INVESTOR
AND THE PUBLIC INTEREST

Since 1949, when President Harry Truman launched the postwar stockpile program, successive Administrations of both parties have concurred in the building of a stockpile of strategic materials for use in a national emergency. For an outlay of $3.5 billion, the government bought materials worth some $12.5 billion at 1981 prices. Even so, the stockpile met only about 50 percent of its legislated goals.

The Reagan Administration clearly would like to expand the stockpile but surely will be constrained by budgetary considerations from making large new commitments to stockpile expansion. The Administration, with its philosophical commitment to free-market principles, might well conclude that the national interest will be served by encouraging private investors to buy and hold strategic materials to be available for government allocation in a national emergency.

To this end, the federal government might logically offer tax incentives to encourage industry and private investors to build nongovernment stockpiles of critical materials. For industry, such incentives might include substantial acceleration of depreciation allowances and investment tax credits. Together these two provisions could offer private, mineral-consuming industries a powerful incentive to expand their inventories for future consumption.

Application of graduated tax incentives would provide benefits for retention of supplies to cover requirements for several years—a form of accumulation quite difficult when interest rates are sky-high. Corporations would be encouraged to finance these inventories through the issuance of bonds secured by the mineral inventories and by enjoying tax benefits similar to those provided by municipal bonds. These corporate bonds would be very attractive to investors because of their tax incentives and their mineral collateral, and would therefore command lower coupon rates, solving the problem of money availability and cost.

Tax benefits could also be made available to the private investor. Those benefits could take the form of lower taxes on capital gains on minerals in which the U.S. government has stockpile requirements. Investors' inventory should be subject to depreciation allowances. Mineral stockpiles on which these benefits were available should be stored in the taxpayer's country of citizenship in order to qualify, whether that country be the U.S. or one of its Free World allies.

The stored materials would be subject to nationalization in time of emergency. The legislation setting up these provisions should clearly define an emergency in which the materials would be taken over by the government, and should clearly set forth the method and timing of payment. Further tax incentives should be applied in case of a national emergency and nationalization of private stockpiles.

The most legitimate purpose of tax incentives and tax shelters is to stimulate investment in areas of industry in which risk and national need exist, but in which a capital base is lacking or deficient. During a recession, demand so created should not overly distort markets. Can there be a more legitimate application of the tax shelter principle than maintaining the independence of the Free World or preventing mass unemployment in industries that would be severely damaged by a minerals embargo?

Investors and industry executives who see merit in these positions might wish to make their views known to their representatives in Congress and to the White House. The authors believe that legislation to encourage private stockpiling would clearly enhance national security at minimal cost to the Treasury in forgone tax receipts, and with far less impact on inflationary pressures than by expansion of the federal deficit to finance government stockpiles with borrowed money.

The actions suggested here seem to be clearly in harmony with the philosophy of the Reagan Administration and with the tone of the Congress and the U.S. electorate.

11

How the Market Works

Investors who are accustomed to owning and trading stocks, bonds and commodity futures will discover new techniques, a new vocabulary and new ways of thinking when they invest in strategic metals. These materials are not just pieces of paper but are tangible commodities, and from the moment a purchaser concludes a trade, he is the legal owner of an identifiable lot of a very real asset with true utility and value.

James Gourlay, an experienced London-based metals broker and a partner in James Sinclair Ltd. of London, has outlined some of the practices and systems that have evolved in the City of London, for many years the world trading center for many of the widely traded industrial metals as well as for the more exotic "minor metals," a designation that includes many of the strategic metals.

For most of these metals, there are two prices to consider, the producer price and a dealer or free-market price. This is also true of platinum and silver, strategic metals that are traded in physical form in London and as futures contracts in U.S. commodity exchanges.

The producer price is the price that a mining company quotes in dealing with large-volume industrial purchasers acquiring metal under long-term fixed-price contracts. The dealer or free-market quotation is the price quoted on an exchange or used in dealer-to-dealer transactions.

The producer price and the free-market or dealer price often vary considerably from each other. At times the producer price may be well above the free-market price, usually in times when the metal is in oversupply; sometimes the more volatile free-market price rises well above the producer price. This is usually an indication that the product is in short supply.

The market behavior of cobalt in 1981 provides an example of the divergence between producer and free-market prices. In the early part of the year, the producer price charged by SOZACOM, the mineral marketing arm of the Zairian government, was $25 a pound;

this fell later in the year to $20 a pound as a worldwide recession reduced demand for cobalt and thus its price. During the year, the free-market price of cobalt was as low as $8.70 a pound.

Similarly, the producer price for platinum remained stable at $475 a troy ounce through most of the year, even while the constantly fluctuating cash or market price ranged from $594 to $375 an ounce.

The purchaser of a strategic metal naturally wishes to get the most advantageous price, but the small or nonindustrial purchaser rarely has the option of buying at the producer price when that quotation is lower than the dealer price. In these conditions, the producers have committed all of their production under long-term contracts and have no more metal to sell. The new buyer has no option but to participate at the higher dealer or free-market price.

Because of the nature of the metals market, it is rarely advisable for a purchaser to enter an order "at the market." He is more likely to enter an order on a "fill or kill" basis—that is, to specify a price limit beyond which he will not go. If the order cannot be filled immediately at the specified price or better, it is canceled.

From experience and daily contact with the market a broker knows a certain number of merchant-dealers who have material in stock and are likely to be able to offer it at advantageous prices. He normally calls two or three merchants or dealers to ask for price indications. Having confirmed which of the two or three dealers is making the best offer, he asks that dealer to make his offer firm. He then checks this offer with one of the others and sometimes further with a second, third or fourth. The broker would then respond with a firm bid to the dealer offering the most favorable price. If the first dealer to whom the broker bids declines the offer, the broker would try others.

This process can go on for some time until the broker is able to buy from one of the dealers, depending upon the overall quantity of material required and the quantities offered by each dealer. As soon as buyer and seller have agreed to a purchase, the broker sends a telex message to the dealer confirming quantity, material and quality, price, method of packing, place of delivery, time of delivery and payment terms. He will shortly receive from the supplier a similar telex confirming the deal. He will then issue an official contract of sale and will receive in due course the seller's official contract of sale.

It should be noted that all of these trades are made on a principal net basis; that is, there is no commission calculated and paid between dealers. Each dealer tends to specialize in certain materials and to develop a network of suppliers and consumers with whom he regularly trades. The role of regular consumers may be of significance even to a customer entering the market, since a regular consumer may be in temporary oversupply, and willing to resell a quantity of metal to the dealer who provided it in the first instance.

It follows therefore that in times of shortage, when the free-market price is higher than the producer price, the consumer will accept the maximum quantity available under his long-term contract with the mining producer, and dispose of any surplus on the free market, establishing a profit for himself in the process.

The producer does not like or approve of this type of dealing, but there is very little he can do about it, especially since in most cases he learns about the dealings, if at all, only long after the event. By then, market conditions will usually have changed.

DOCUMENTATION

Under the customs prevailing in London, a number of documents will be issued to the purchaser of a batch or lot of metal. While the procedures are less rigid than in the stock and commodity exchanges of the U.S., it is highly advisable for investors doing business in London to follow the customary procedures there and to use the assaying and sampling services approved by the London Metal Exchange. The following documents will be issued:

1. Confirmation of sale, issued by the broker to the client, confirming the materials purchased, quantity, minimum grade, price and commission.

2. Warehouse receipt, issued by the warehouse, stating the amount and type of material being held.

3. Sampling certificate, issued by an inspector, documenting a sight inspection and weighing of the material in the warehouse.

4. Assayer's report, based on a chemical analysis of the material stored, showing its exact chemical compositions and degree of purity.

5. Audit report, based on an annual audit by a firm of auditors retained through the client's broker. Copies of the audit report confirming the presence of physical materials deposited in a warehouse

and insured against fire, theft and other hazards. In most cases, this warehouse will be located in Rotterdam, Holland, and the net price of the materials to the investor will be free in the warehouse. If the buyer wishes to take delivery in another warehouse, he will be billed for any additional delivery costs.

Normally, delivery will take place in 30 to 90 days after the trade date. If immediate delivery is required, a premium may be charged. The client has the choice of accepting delivery of the warehouse receipt and accompanying reports or he may ask his broker to retain these documents. We strongly recommend that the client take possession of his receipts and reports. If the receipt is held by the broker, it should be insured for full value against loss, and the client should receive a reference duplicate of the receipt, the assay report, and the sampling report.

Storage and insurance. The materials will be held in a warehouse and must be insured. Storage and insurance charges will be payable in the customary currency of the warehouse and the insurance company. Storage charges are generally paid annually, while insurance charges are payable monthly. Most brokers will handle these details for you if you wish, at a monthly maintenance fee of about 0.25 percent of the initial purchase price, billed quarterly.

Charges. The principal amount of the cost of the materials will be billed to the client's account on the basis of the standard unit size, and afterward the client's account will be credited or debited for small variations in the actual amount of the material delivered. These variances are generally within 2 percent of the unit size originally ordered. In the case of a material purchased in alloy or oxide form, the client will pay the quoted price times the percentage of the pure material contained in the alloy or oxide.

The broker will charge a sales commission. In addition, the warehouse will charge for accepting and segregating the client's materials within its storage area. These delivery charges will usually not exceed $75 per unit and will be paid by the broker and passed on to the buyer.

The sampling charge made by the inspector for sampling inspection at the warehouse will vary with the amount of material inspected, and usually will not exceed $100 per unit. An assaying charge for the chemical analysis of the material will usually not exceed $150 per unit. These charges will be passed on by the broker to the buyer. If the buyer prefers to have his broker arrange these details, the cost of storage, insurance, and annual inspection will be covered typically by the charge mentioned earlier, about 0.25 percent a month of the total original cost of the material. As mentioned, this charge will generally be billed quarterly.

The following table shows the customary unit sizes and storage requirements for some of the strategic metals:

Material	Unit Size	Form	Packing	Quality
Antimony	5 metric tons	Ingots	Wooden cases	99.6% min. purity 0.15% max. arsenic
Beryllium	2,500 kilos	Beryllium-copper alloy	Drums	Approx. 4% beryllium content
Cadmium	2 metric tons	2″-diameter balls, sticks or ingots	Wooden cases or drums	99.95% min. purity
Chromium	1 metric ton	Lumps	Steel drums	99.0% min. purity
Cobalt	250 kilos	Broken cathodes	Steel drums	99.6% min. purity
Columbium	2 metric tons	Ferro-columbium	Drums	60–70% columbium
Electro-manganese	10 metric tons	Flakes	Steel drums	99.95% min. purity
Gallium	30 kilos	Semiliquid	Plastic bottles	99.9% min. purity
Germanium	20 kilos	Ingots	Wooden boxes	99.99% min. purity 50 ohm resistivity
Hafnium	100 kilos	Sponge	Poly bottles	99.99% min. purity
Indium	50 kilos	Ingots	Drums	99.99% min. purity

Material	Unit Size	Form	Packing	Quality
Lithium	500 kilos	Ingots	Watertight containers	99.9% min. purity
Magnesium	5 metric tons	Ingots	Shrink wrapped	99.8% min. purity
Mercury	50 flasks	Liquid	Flasks of 76 lb.	99.99% min. purity
Molybdenum	1,500 kilos	Molybdenum-oxide powder	Tins or drums (N.B. tins smaller than drums)	Mo 55–65%
Rhodium	20 troy oz.	Sponge	Plastic bottles	99.90% min. purity
Selenium	1,000 kilos	Powder (–200 mesh)	Wooden cases	99.5% min. purity
Silicon	10 metric tons	Irregular lumps, 10 to 100 mm.	Metal boxes or drums	99.85% min. purity
Tantalite	200 lbs.	Ta_2O_5 ore	Bags/drums	60% min. Ta_2O_5
Tellurium	500 kilos	Small ingots	Wooden cases	99.7% min. purity
Titanium	500 kilos	Sponge (irregular granules) T.G. 100 brand or equivalent	Drums	99.6% typical purity
Tungsten	1 metric ton	Concentrate ore	Drums	65–70% WO_3
Vanadium	2 metric tons	Ferro-vanadium	Drums	50–60% Vanadium
Zirconium	10 metric tons	Powdered concentrated ore	Drums	Varies with end use

Note: 1 metric ton = 1000 kilograms (kilos) = 2,204.6 pounds.

READING THE MARKETS

Traders in stocks and bonds become attuned to reading the day's events in terms of how those developments will affect the markets. Metal prices also respond to economic trends, geopolitical developments and technological change. The experienced metal trader learns to read the news with close regard for its effect upon his investments.

Factors Negative to Price

Global recession. The International Monetary Fund forecasts little or no real economic growth through the early 1980s and possibly to 1985. The most negative case one can make in real terms for commercial metals is a deflationary period without real growth. In this case, most strategic metals would rise only to reflect increased costs of mining and refining, while metals with large outstanding inventories or decreasing technological applications would decline in price until approaching parity with alternative substitutes.

Complete normalization of relations with South Africa and secured access to its minerals. The Reagan Administration has quietly sought to improve relations with Pretoria without ending its participation in the U.N. sanctions against arms shipments to South Africa, virtually ensuring that the South Africans will not place an embargo on movement of strategic materials to the U.S. and the West, but the possibility of internal disturbances that might interfere with the production and shipment of minerals cannot be dismissed.

Shelving of European stockpile plans. West Germany, the United Kingdom and Spain have all dropped, for the present, plans to pursue aggressive national stockpiling programs. This has had a temporary negative effect on the market.

Stockpile sales. The managers of the U.S. strategic stockpile occasionally dispose of materials judged to be in surplus, and such sales usually have a depressing effect on prices of specific metals. Stockpile sales, real and prospective, depressed tin and silver prices in 1981.

Factors Positive to Price

Aggressive actions by the USSR. As the National Strategy Information Center pointed out in a 1980 White Paper,[1] the Soviet Union has continued since the end of the Vietnam war to extend its influence into mineral-rich areas of the Third World. Cuban troops and East German advisors remain in Ethiopia, where they played a decisive role in driving the forces of Somalia out of the disputed region of Ogaden in 1978. From Ethiopia, they are within striking distance of the oil-rich Arabian peninsula and the sea-lanes linking it to the West.

In Southern Africa, another contingent of Cuban troops aided by Soviet and East German advisors help to ensure continued Marxist control of the pivotal state of Angola. That former colony of the Portuguese supports a guerrilla movement aimed at extending Marxist control to neighboring Namibia, and it poses a threat to the surviving free states in the region. Across the neck of Southern Africa another Marxist regime controls Mozambique, its minerals and its ports.

The presence of Marxist governments in Southern Africa tends to sustain international tensions in the region and to keep alive the threat of a Soviet-dominated cartel that could control the two regions of the world richest in strategic minerals, the Soviet Union and Southern Africa.

Increased defense spending by the Reagan Administration. Orders for new weapons systems such as the B-1 bomber, the radar-blinding Stealth bomber, the MX missile and the new cruise missiles, as well as a general strengthening and upgrading of older systems, will increase demand for defense-related metals. Most market analysts feel that the prospect of accelerated defense spending has not yet been reflected in metal prices.

Stockpiling. The Administration's stockpiling intentions are not yet (in early 1982) reflected in legislation or substantial appropriations. Any large acquisitions for the stockpile will positively affect metal prices.

A STRATEGIC BALANCE

A careful examination of the positive and negative factors in the market will provide the strategic investor with the properly balanced viewpoint in making investment decisions. We conclude that strategic materials should occupy 15 percent of an investment portfolio, broken down to commit:

1. 5 percent based on geopolitical considerations,

2. 5 percent based on economic considerations and
3. 5 percent based on market timing disciplines.

How an individual investor allocates his funds is, in part, a matter of personal taste and inclination. Investors accustomed to dealing in physical metals, especially the precious metals, may feel at home in the world of strategics, where physical metals wholly owned are the standard form of commitment. Investors who still prefer to deal in dividend-paying securities may prefer to buy common stocks in producing companies; these offer an alternative form of participation that could prove rewarding.

FRAMEWORK FOR ANALYSIS

Here are some of the factors to consider before committing funds to an investment in strategic metals.

1. *Demand outlook.* Are basic uses for the material increasing or declining? Are the industries in which it is used expected to grow or stagnate? Would the material benefit from stockpile purchases?

2. *Supply outlook.* Is supply of the material threatened by geopolitical interruption? Are existing extraction and processing companies expanding or contracting, producing more or less material? Is there a large inventory overhanging the market?

3. *Substitutes.* Are there alternate materials available that can be substituted for the investment metal at reasonable prices and delivering reasonable performance? Can substitutes be introduced under known engineering principles?

4. *Price.* Is the material at an all-time high or is it at historically low levels? What is the relationship between the producer price and the free-market price?

RECOMMENDATIONS

With appreciation for the market and geopolitical conditions prevailing in early 1982, these specific materials may be recommended for purchase:

Primary group: Chromium, cobalt, germanium, manganese.
Secondary group: Antimony, indium, rhodium, titanium.

The Metals

Chromium is the classic indispensable metal in modern industry. Most of it is produced in politically sensitive areas of Southern Africa

(South Africa and Zimbabwe) or the Soviet Union. These three nations accounted for 78 percent of world production in 1981 and 98 percent of known world mineral reserves. The great preponderance of new reserves discovered between 1975 and 1980 was found in Southern Africa.

American mining firms seeking government help to explore marginal deposits in Oregon and Northern California have found little to encourage them. Reportedly, a high-level Bureau of Mines official advised one mining executive: "You'd be better off to put your money in the bank and to sit on the beach in Florida and collect the interest."

Chromium is totally essential for the making of stainless steel, which is used in a wide range of industrial and military applications. Chromium is one of the metals likely to be acquired for the strategic stockpile when and if the Administration launches an aggressive purchasing program, since it is virtually irreplaceable as a military metal, and stockpile inventories are far below their goals. Because of a worldwide slowdown in steelmaking, consumption of chromium in 1981 was the lowest since 1975, suggesting that a buying opportunity developed.

Manganese is used mainly in the manufacture of steel, iron and aluminum. In the making of steel it is irreplaceable: without manganese there is no steel. The U.S. is 98 percent dependent upon imports, and its principal suppliers are Gabon, South Africa, Australia and Brazil.

Attempted price hikes by producers within the past two years have been met with resistance by recession-ridden steelmakers. With U.S. stockpile inventory at 88 percent of its goal, stockpiling will not have a major effect on prices in the near future. We recommend purchases of manganese because there are no substitutes and because of the U.S.'s high dependence upon imports.

Cobalt is recommended for purchase because of its importance for defense and for general industrial uses and because of the possibility of supply interruptions in the future. Cobalt is an irreplaceable component of steels used in jet aircraft engines, and extremely useful in metallurgical and chemical applications. Prices have fluctuated from a high close to $50 a pound on the spot market in 1978 to a late 1981 low of $8.70 a pound. The federal government is buying cobalt for the stockpile. Limited production of cobalt from the Blackbird mine in Idaho may resume in the mid-1980s if suitable price supports can be worked out.

Germanium is a metal or metalloid used in electronics and in lasers, in infrared optics and in fiber optic technology. The market for germanium is small and volatile, carrying high risk and the potential for high reward. The USSR, which formerly was a major supplier to the world market, changed in 1980 from a net seller to a net buyer with the purpose, by some educated guesses, of equipping its growing tank fleet with night sights. Germanium is a trace element usually found in zinc ores, and production is controlled more by the output of zinc than by direct demand for germanium. In 1981 the price for imported germanium ranged as high as $950 a kilogram, and there were suspicions, never proved, that the erratic price behavior resulted in part from an attempt to corner the market in an element of which only 125,000 kilograms were produced in all the world in 1981.

Antimony, a metal formerly used mainly as a hardener for lead grids in automobile storage batteries, is finding increased demand in the manufacture of flameproofing compounds. It is also used in bullets, camouflage paint, smoke bombs and the manufacture of glass and ceramics. The People's Republic of China is the world's principal producer of antimony, and almost 60 percent of the world's known reserve is located there. U.S. demand is expected to rise by 3 percent a year, and the price behavior of antimony is likely to depend upon the rate of exports from China.

Indium is attractive as an investment/speculation because of its growing applications in electronics and the prospect of its greatly expanded use in solar power generation. World production of indium in 1981 was estimated at 1,400,000 troy ounces (about 43,500 kilograms), and this output is unlikely to increase suddenly because production depends upon the recovery of trace amounts from zinc and other base metal ores. The price action in indium has been erratic in recent years, and successful investment will depend largely upon success in buying in a favorable price range. Dealer sales at around $20 an ounce ($623 a kilogram) were reported in 1981.

Rhodium, one of the platinum group of metals, shares the high prices of the other precious metals. Its principal uses are in catalytic converters, anticorrosive coatings and optical instruments. South Africa and the USSR together produce some 90 percent of the world supply of rhodium; the U.S. is dependent upon imports for about 93 percent of its needs. Because its supply is limited and its uses many, rhodium merits a recommendation to buy when its price is in an attractive range.

Titanium derives its major importance as a high-strength low-weight structural metal for airframes and jet engines, military and civilian. It is used in other aerospace applications. Spurred by prices that ranged as high as $22 a kilo for sponge in 1979–80, production capacity in the U.S. and Japan was expanded, and in the U.S. capacity will continue to come on line until 1986. Imports of titanium from the USSR ceased in July 1980; some experts believe that the Soviets were allocating much of their production to the construction of titanium-hulled submarines. Because of a lag in civilian aircraft production, the price of sponge declined in early 1982 to around $10 a kilo. A new surge in aircraft production for civilian or military purposes could place new demands on the titanium supply and upward pressure on prices.

Portfolios

Because strategic metals held in inventory produce no current income, most investors find it inadvisable to commit more than 15 percent of their investable funds in such purchases. Within those guidelines, the following portfolios offer some diversification and the prospect of price appreciation over a holding period of three to five years.

Material	Lot Size	No. Lots
$16,000 investment		
Chromium	1 metric ton	1
Manganese	10 metric tons	1
$21,000 investment		
Chromium	1 metric ton	1
Manganese	10 metric tons	1
Cobalt	250 kilos	1
$37,000 investment (primary portfolio)		
Chromium	1 metric ton	1
Manganese	10 metric tons	1
Cobalt	250 kilos	1
Germanium	20 kilos	1
$40,000 investment		
Chromium	1 metric ton	1
Manganese	10 metric tons	1

Material	Lot Size	No. Lots
Cobalt	250 kilos	1
Germanium	20 kilos	1
Titanium	500 kilos	1

$51,000 investment (complete portfolio)

Chromium	1 metric ton	1
Manganese	10 metric tons	1
Cobalt	250 kilos	1
Germanium	20 kilos	1
Titanium	500 kilos	1
Antimony	5 metric tons	1
Rhodium	20 troy ounces	1
Indium	50 kilos	1

$83,000 investment

Chromium	1 metric ton	2
Manganese	10 metric tons	2
Cobalt	250 kilos	2
Germanium	20 kilos	1
Titanium	500 kilos	1
Antimony	5 metric tons	1
Rhodium	20 troy ounces	1
Indium	50 kilos	1

Note: Designing portfolios is a highly individual process. It is important to discuss your investment needs and the current market conditions with a qualified representative before committing to purchase contracts. The portfolios shown above are samples only. Grade, delivery and other specifications should be worked out according to procedures outlined earlier in this chapter.

12

Strategic Investments in Common Shares

As the preceding chapters have made clear, an investor interested in the concept of strategic metals has a variety of investments from which to choose. The actual ownership of strategic metals will be a new experience for many, and perhaps a little unsettling to those much more accustomed to owning paper securities such as stocks and bonds. For such investors, the shares in companies producing, processing or marketing strategic metals may offer interesting opportunities to participate in the bull market in strategics that seems likely to develop during the 1980s.

Ownership of common shares in these companies offers some familiar advantages. Most of the shares yield dividends, some quite generous. Prices of most of the shares are listed on the major stock exchanges or published in special columns in the leading financial dailies, and the markets in the main are liquid, meaning that a shareholder can add to or liquidate his investments on any business day. Thus, it is possible to respond quickly and effectively to changing geopolitical situations. This liquidity also creates opportunities for short-term trading profits, although success is more likely to reward those who buy and hold for two to five years.

In our view, the best opportunity for profit lies in taking advantage of the full inventory accumulation cycle, buying in the period when shares (or physical metals) are out of demand, holding the securities to the top of the demand cycle, and selling at a profit.

We have explained that metals basically respond to realities. One of the realities of the early 1980s was that in a worldwide industrial recession, demand was off for many of the strategic metals, which are also basic industrial raw materials. In the absence of a true international crisis threatening the supply of critical and strategic materials, prices sagged, depressing corporate profits and stock prices of the producing companies. With industrial recovery, demand and prices will rise again, boosting sales, profits and share prices. This

148

familiar cyclical behavior is predictable even in the absence of a raw materials crisis that would accompany any major East-West or North-South confrontation.

All stock markets react in some degree to geopolitical developments, but shares in strategic-metal producers react more sharply than most. Futures markets are even more sensitive to such developments, and professional or nonprofessional traders familiar with the behavior of futures markets can easily transfer their expertise to the field of strategics. But except for silver, platinum and copper, which are commonly traded commodities as well as strategic metals, there are no functional futures markets open to public participation. So following the axiom that an investor should remain true to his profile and operate where he is comfortable, a metals trader may wish to continue to deal in physical metals. A seasoned futures trader may concentrate on the futures markets for silver, platinum and copper, while the much larger group of common share investors may wish to stick with securities they are accustomed to trading—common stocks.

The shares that we will describe will not be as familiar to the typical reader and investor as, say, AT&T or IBM, but they will be widely traded stocks with more liquid markets than the underlying physical metals. In general, the shares of the companies will move in response to the markets for the primary products, but because of the leverage effect, they may react even more decisively than metal prices. The shares will be easier to buy and sell through any major securities firm dealing in U.S. and international securities or any major bank dealing in international investments. The equity in South African companies will be represented by American Depository Receipts (ADRs), which entitle the holder to receive dividends but not to vote in the affairs of the company; that privilege is reserved under South African law to residents of South Africa. Unlike the physical metals, the shares offer no problems in assaying, storage and insurance, and transfer and brokerage costs will be lower than for an equivalent investment in physical metals.

As with direct investments in metals, we recommend the purchase of portfolios of securities rather than placing all one's investable resources in a single company or a single metal.

Shares offer the additional advantage of discounting future growth. While the price of a metal tends to reflect immediate day-to-day demand for the product, the price of shares reflects the market's expectations of future profits as well. Common shares are by nature a discounting device, tending to take into account the public's expectations as well as present conditions. Thus political events, economic trends and government policies and promises that affect the markets for strategic metals will have a geometric rather than a simple arithmetic effect on the companies in the field. This must be understood as a double-edged sword. The shares thus present the best avenue for taking advantage of market leverage—realizing present profit for future values.

THE SHARES

Because most of the companies producing or processing strategic metals are involved in the marketing of other products as well, very few companies represent a pure play in strategic metals. This is true for North American as well as for South African and Australian companies.

In North America, the purest play in strategics is Oregon Metallurgical (traded over-the-counter), which earns 85 percent of its revenues from making titanium sponge—the basic refined material for fabricating machined parts of titanium metal. Allegheny International, a large company identified mainly with the production of specialty steels, is also involved in titanium and other strategic metals, and it holds substantial investments in South African metallurgical ventures.

Among other companies that earn substantial revenues from strategic metals are Teledyne Inc., Cabot Corp. and Teck Corp. Teledyne, based in Los Angeles, produces zirconium, tungsten, columbium, molybdenum and alloy steels, realizing about 27 percent of its revenues from its specialty-metals division. The Boston-based Cabot Corp. is a diversified company earning about one-third of its revenues from strategic products including cobalt and nickel-based alloys. Through a Canadian affiliate Cabot is a producer of tantalum, and through another affiliate it trades in London in beryllium, cobalt, chromium, tantalum and titanium. Teck Corp. of Vancouver, B.C., is the largest miner of columbium in North America, although its revenues in columbium are overshadowed by those from its large gold, silver and zinc operations.

U.S. Antimony Co. is the largest independent U.S. producer of antimony, a strategic metal for which demand may increase for car batteries and for a variety of military uses. Consolidated Durham, based in Toronto, also mines antimony and is of possible interest to investors in strategic metals.

In the American West, efforts are under way to develop deposits of metals in which the U.S. is almost totally import-dependent. In Idaho, Noranda Mines, a subsidiary of a Canadian mining company, is attempting to reopen and redevelop the Blackbird mine for the production of cobalt. In the Stillwater region of Montana, the Johns-Manville Corp. and its partner, Chevron Oil, were attempting to develop a large deposit of platinum-palladium ore. Start-up costs in both the Blackbird cobalt mine and the Stillwater complex will be enormous, and the mines are not expected to operate profitably for several years.

Outside North America, the most obvious field for share investment in strategics is South Africa, the Free World's principal supplier for a long list of critical and strategic metals. South African Manganese Corp. and the Associated Manganese Corp. are the world's number one and two producers of manganese. Both companies also manufacture steel and market much of their manganese output in the form of steel. They are exporters of ferromanganese, the intermediate product between ore and manganese metal and the material used in the manufacture of steel.

Transvaal Consolidated Lands Investment Co. is a large producer of chromium, but chromium represents only a minor proportion of its total mineral production. Rustenberg Platinum is the Free World's leading producer of platinum group metals, and also produces some cobalt as a by-product of its platinum metal recovery.

Australia is emerging as another major supplier of strategic metals, principally titanium, vanadium, bauxite and cadmium. The most obvious way to participate in these industries is through ownership of stock in the largest mining companies, such as Western Mining Corp. and MIM Holdings Ltd. These companies also are engaged in oil and gas exploration.

As a rule, North American companies operate in relatively small ore deposits (Inco Ltd. of Canada, the world's largest producer of nickel, is an exception to this rule), but they profit from a climate of political stability. They are cyclical industries, keyed to industrial demand in North America and Europe. The mines of South Africa tend to be far larger and richer and their recovery costs minimal; they are highly competitive and are supported by an efficient infrastructure of roads, railroads and power supply. They have the capital and the technology to upgrade their product, that is to process such ores as manganese and chromium into the more valuable ferromanganese and ferrochrome for export, or to incorporate them into steel for export. The cloud overhanging South Africa is the political outlook, the prospect that racial conflict may in the future impair the nation's ability to produce and export its minerals. Even taking into account this possibility, the shares in South African mines would appear to offer promising prospects for present and future capital gains.

Australia's natural resources are impressive, but for an odd psychological reason, Australia is the last of the major mining countries to share in market booms. There is a cliché about Australian securities that when they peak, the boom is over.

The following brief research reports on individual companies were compiled by Martin McNeill, senior vice-president and head of the equities department of Sinclair Securities Co. Mr. McNeill also drafted the proposed model portfolios of common shares in strategic metals companies.

NORTH AMERICAN COMPANIES

Allegheny International

Shares outstanding (millions):   10.2
Share price movements, 1981–mid-'82:   55–23*

Allegheny International (formerly Allegheny Ludlum) is a diversified company producing specialty metals and alloys, and a range of industrial and consumer products. Specialty metals include superalloys and nickel and cobalt base alloys for aerospace and power generating uses. The company also owns 50 percent of Titanium Metals Corp. of America, and mining and metallurgical interests in South Africa.

Amax Inc.

Shares outstanding (millions):   62.7
Share price movements, 1981–mid-'82:   69–18*

A diversified natural resources company, Amax is the world's leading producer of molybdenum, and has interests in base metals, silver, coal, oil, aluminum and iron ore.

*All prices are in U.S. dollars.

Cabot Corp.

Shares outstanding (millions):   31.4
Share price movements, 1981–mid-'82: 36–16*

The Cabot Corp. is a diversified producer of energy, raw materials and chemicals; it is the largest domestic producer of carbon black. Cabot owns a 35 percent interest in Tantalum Mining Corp. of Canada and trades in cobalt, chromium, tantalum and titanium through a London subsidiary.

Consolidated Durham

Shares outstanding (millions):   7.5
Share price range, 1981–mid-'82:   5–.50*

Toronto-based Consolidated Durham is North America's largest producer of antimony, and expects to increase production by bringing a new mine into production during 1982. Another ore body developed by Consolidated Durham contains tungsten and molybdenum as well as antimony. The company also has gold and silver properties at Yankee Fork, Idaho.

Falconbridge Nickel

Shares outstanding (millions):   5.2
Share price movements, 1981–mid-'82: 105–25*

Falconbridge Nickel Mines Ltd., based in Toronto, is an integrated mining company operating in Canada, Norway, the Dominican Republic and Africa. Its products include nickel, ferronickel, cobalt, copper, other base metals and some silver and gold.

Hemisphere Development Corp.

Shares outstanding (millions):   2.3
Share price movements 1981–mid-'82: 15–2*

Hemisphere Development is a small but relatively successful oil and gas company that has three mineral properties under development involving tantalum, lithium, tungsten and gold, all in Canada's Northwest Territories.

*All prices are in U.S. dollars.

Inco Inc.

Shares outstanding (millions):   76.7
Share price movements, 1981–mid-'82:   24–8*

Inco, a Canadian company, produces some 30 percent of the non-Communist world's nickel, as well as copper and other base metals and some precious metals. It is also a manufacturer of automobile batteries and dry-cell batteries, and through its subsidiary Inco Alloy, markets high-nickel alloys.

Nord Resources

Shares outstanding (millions):   4.2
Share price movements, 1981–mid-'82:   25–8*

Nord Resources is a U.S.-based company whose principal business is the production of kaolin, an industrial mineral used to coat paper. It also owns a chrome-cobalt-nickel mining property in Papua New Guinea, and a 15 percent interest in a titanium-mining venture in Sierra Leone in west Africa.

Nuclear Metals

Shares outstanding (millions):   2.6
Share price movements, 1981–mid-'82:   26–10*

This company manufactures metal products using metallurgical technology developed by the company and its predecessors. It is engaged in the production of metal powders, parts of depleted uranium and an assortment of specialty-metal parts. Nuclear Metals expects that its titanium alloy and nickel- and cobalt-based alloy powders will increase in importance in the future.

Oregon Metallurgical

Shares outstanding (millions):   15.1
Share price range, 1981–mid-'82:   40–9*

Oregon Metallurgical processes titanium sponge and scrap into metal and alloys for aircraft, missiles, rockets and other applications where titanium's high strength-to-weight ratio is vital. The company

*All prices are in U.S. dollars.

is the purest play in strategic metals. About 80 percent of its shares are owned by Armco Inc.

United States Antimony

Shares outstanding (millions): 4.9
Share price movements, 1981–mid-'82: 9–2.75*

The company's principal business is mining, milling and refining antimony ore in Montana and producing antimony products. It also has a silver-gold operation in Idaho and interests in several other mining ventures.

SOUTH AFRICAN COMPANIES

Associated Manganese

Shares outstanding (millions): 3.5
Share price range, 1981–mid-'82: 100–52*

Associated Manganese is South Africa's second largest producer of manganese (after South African Manganese). It is controlled by Anglovaal, and represents 20 percent of Anglovaal's holdings.

Consolidated Murchison

Shares outstanding (millions): 3.5
Share price range, 1981–mid-'82: 14–2*

Consolidated Murchison is one of the world's largest producers of antimony. In early 1982, it announced a 30 percent reduction in output because of poor market conditions.

General Mining Union Corp. (Gencor)

Shares outstanding (millions): 42
Share price range, 1981–mid-'82: 39–10*

Gencor is one of the most powerful of the South African mining-finance houses with widely diversified interests in the industry. Through operating subsidiaries, it is responsible for the production of 24 percent of South Africa's uranium, 40 percent of its platinum, as well as 40 percent of its coal and 16 percent of its gold.

*All prices are in U.S. dollars.

Highveld Steel & Vanadium

Shares outstanding (millons):   67.9
Share price range, 1981–mid-'82:   6–2.5*

Highveld Steel & Vanadium is a vertically integrated producer of vanadium, an element used in alloying steel for use in machine tools, jet engines, pipelines and rail steel. South Africa is taking a commanding position in world trade in vanadium, and Highveld is the major factor in the industry.

Impala Platinum

Shares outstanding (millions):   57
Share price range, 1981–mid-'82:   11–3*

Impala is the second-largest platinum producer in the Western world, ranking after its South African neighbor, Rustenburg. Impala's reserves have been estimated as sufficient to sustain production at the rate of more than one million ounces of platinum a year for 25 years, assuming prices at the level of mid-1978 ($220 an ounce).

Johannesburg Consolidated Investments

Shares outstanding (millions):   7.1
Share price range, 1981–mid-'82:   125–34*

Johannesburg Consolidated (Johnnies) ranks as one of the most interesting of the mining-finance companies with a broad range of holdings in mining, brewing and real estate. Through its investments it is involved in the mining of platinum, diamonds and gold, and in the production of ferrochrome. It is active in exploration, suggesting that it will continue to be a major factor in South African mining.

Rustenburg Platinum Holdings

Share outstanding (millions):   125
Share price range, 1981–mid-'82:   8–2*

Rustenburg Platinum is certainly the Western world's largest producer of platinum and is probably the world leader as well. It operates three major mines in South Africa's Transvaal province, producing platinum as well as palladium, rhodium, ruthenium, iridium,

---

*All prices are in U.S. dollars.

osmium, gold, silver, copper and nickel. *Mining Journal* of London observes: "The strong financial position and the greater flexibility which has been built into the operations in the last few years places shareholders in a position to benefit rapidly from any improvement in metal markets. The extensive life of operations adds to the shares' merit."

South Africa Manganese (Samancor)

Shares outstanding (millions):   27.8
Share price range, 1981–mid-'82:   5–1*

Samancor is the world's largest exporter of manganese and ferromanganese and is also a significant producer of ferrochrome. It has massive ore reserves, highly efficient furnaces and access to cheap coal-based energy. A Wall Street analyst reports: "Samancor is benefiting from a worldwide restructuring of the ferro-alloy business. The conversion process is energy-intensive, and there have been substantial technical changes recently, particularly in ferrochrome. . . . Predominance is passing to cheap-energy countries like South Africa, which draws most of its power from abundant local coal."

AUSTRALIAN COMPANIES

MIM Holdings (ADRs)

Shares outstanding (millions):   22.3
Share price movements, 1981–mid-'82:   17–2*

MIM is a major producer of silver, lead, zinc and copper with a growing range of diversified interests. It participates in a nickel project in western Australia and is involved in mining and exploration for coal, and in oil exploration in Australia and Papua New Guinea.

Western Mining

Shares outstanding (millions):   16.3
Share price movements, 1981–mid-'82   7–3*

Western mining is Australia's largest precious metal and base metal conglomerate, owning major interests in Australia's most active mines. With the U.S.'s General Dynamics, it is building a titanium sponge plant.

*All prices are in U.S. dollars.

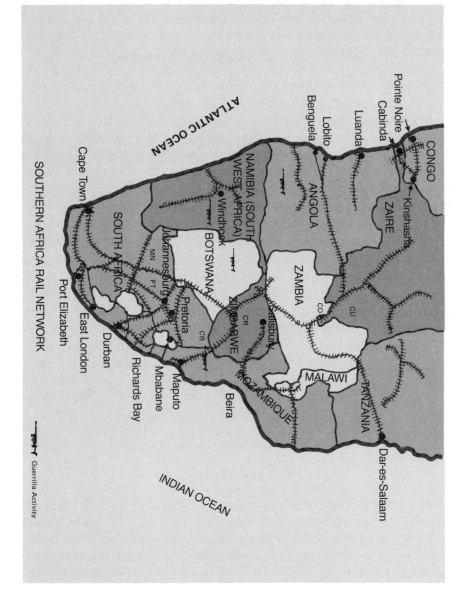

SOUTHERN AFRICA RAIL NETWORK

ATLANTIC OCEAN

INDIAN OCEAN

Guerrilla Activity

Pointe Noire
Cabinda
Benguela
Lobito
Luanda
Kinshasa
CONGO
ZAIRE
ANGOLA
NAMIBIA (SOUTH WEST AFRICA)
Windhoek
BOTSWANA
ZAMBIA
MALAWI
TANZANIA
Dar-es-Salaam
Cape Town
SOUTH AFRICA
Johannesburg
Pretoria
Salisbury
ZIMBABWE
MOZAMBIQUE
Beira
Maputo
Mbabane
Richards Bay
Durban
East London
Port Elizabeth
MN
PT
CR
CR
CO
CU

PORTFOLIOS

Almost any investor prefers to reduce his risk by diversifying rather than concentrating all his resources in one or two companies or a small number of commodities. The authors recommend the commitment of no more than 15 to 20 percent of an investor's available funds in a portfolio of stocks in the field of strategic materials. With that limitation in mind, we present these model portfolios as suggestions only. Prices and market conditions are constantly changing and any investor should consult his broker or investment advisor before making his commitments. The following portfolios are designed to provide diversification among geographical areas (North America, South Africa, Australia) and among the strategic materials the companies produce. Prices are based on June 1982 quotations.

$25,000 Portfolio

Portfolio (percentage)	No. of Shares	Stock	Price	Value
16	200	Cabot Corp.	20	$ 4,000
28.8	800	Inco Ltd.	9	7,200
13.6	100	Johannesburg Consol. Inv.	34	3,400
20	500	Oregon Metallurgical	10	5,000
12	1,000	Highveld Steel & Vanadium	3	3,000
9.6	1,200	Rustenburg Platinum	2	2,400
100.0				$ 25,000

$50,000 Portfolio

Portfolio (percentage)	No. of Shares	Stock	Price	Value
14.4	300	Allegheny Int.	24	$ 7,200
12	300	Cabot Corp.	20	6,000
18	1,000	Inco Ltd.	9	9,000
20	1,000	Oregon Metallurgical	10	10,000
8.8	400	Nuclear Metals	11	4,400
6.8	100	Johannesburg Consol. Inv.	34	3,400
5.4	900	Western Mining	3	2,700
5	2,500	South African Manganese	1	2,500
9.6	2,400	Rustenburg Platinum	2	4,800
100.0				$ 50,000

$100,000 Portfolio

Portfolio (percentage)	No. of Shares	Stock	Price	Value
3.8	200	Amax Inc.	19	$ 3,800
4.8	200	Allegheny Intl.	24	4,800
10	500	Cabot Corp.	20	10,000
18	2,000	Inco Ltd.	9	18,000
5.5	500	Nuclear Metals	11	5,500
10	1,000	General Mining (Gencor)	10	10,000
3.4	100	Johannesburg Consol. Inv.	34	3,400
11	1,100	Oregon Metallurgical	10	11,000
5.8	2,900	Rustenburg Platinum	2	5,800
4.5	4,500	S.A. Manganese Corp.	1	4,500
15	5,000	Highveld Steel & Vanadium	3	15,000
6	2,000	U.S. Antimony	3	6,000
2.2	1,100	MIM Holdings	2	2,200
100.0				$100,000

13

What the Future Holds

The Arab oil embargo of 1973-74 did far more than consign impatient drivers to waiting lines at gas pumps and touch off a revolution among Detroit's auto designers. It served as a chilling reminder of how profoundly America could be damaged by a shortage of one crucial raw material and it raised questions about the security of supply of other critical materials, notably metals from the Third World.

Despite rumblings of discontent from the Third World, production of strategic metals continued largely uninterrupted through the 1970s. Led by Cuba after the Castro revolution, a number of producing countries—notably Zaire, Zambia, Chile and Peru—partially or totally nationalized mining properties in their territory, but except for Cuba, which first took over American-owned nickel mines and then diverted most of their production to the Communist bloc, most of the producing countries continued to sell their minerals to their traditional customers in the industrial West. Even so, some experts in Washington began to worry about the security of America's future supplies of key raw materials. Among those concerned were career professionals in the Bureau of Mines, who follow worldwide developments in mining, and executives of American mining and metallurgical companies.

These businessmen were acutely aware of a deteriorating investment climate in the Third World. Where nationalization had not occurred it was an overhanging threat, and Third World countries were setting an increasingly high price, political and economic, for access to their minerals. The mining companies were also feeling pressures at home, where environmental laws and rules were adding to the cost of doing business and forcing some smelters and mines to close. Environmental groups lobbied for permanent barriers to the exploration and mineral development of public lands. Stop-and-go stockpiling in which large sales from government stocks depressed metal prices further weakened the mining industry.

Some of Washington's foundations and think tanks picked up signals of trouble ahead. Georgetown University's Center for Strategic and International Studies in 1979 published a report by Amos A. Jordon and Robert A. Kilmarx (*Strategic Mineral Dependence: the Stockpile Dilemma*) warning of future mineral supply problems. Other CSIS scholars focused on foreign policy questions from a perspective of mineral dependence. The Council on Economics and National Security produced its own study (*The Resource War and the U.S. Business Community*) and cooperated with the World Affairs Council of Pittsburgh to organize a conference in June 1980 in which panels of experts assessed the strategic implications of the Soviet Union's Resource War against the West.

Several U.S. Senators began to speak out on the minerals issue. South Carolina's Strom Thurmond worried about America's growing dependence upon Southern Africa, while New Mexico's Harrison Schmitt, a professional geologist and former astronaut, and Virginia's John Warner, who had served as secretary of the navy under Richard Nixon, began to work on new legislation. In the House of Representatives, Nevada's Jim Santini, a Congressman with a home-state constituency in mining and a ready-made platform as chairman of the House subcommittee on Mines and Mining, held hearings on mineral problems and in 1980 led a Congressional fact-finding tour through Southern Africa. The subcommittee published two significant reports on its findings.

In time, the issue of mineral dependency began to attract the attention of the press. *Aviation Week and Space Technology,* followed by *Business Week, Time, Fortune* and the major daily newspapers, published articles on the subject. By the time the Reagan Administration arrived in Washington in January 1981 the ground was prepared for new initiatives.

In fact, the legislative framework for government action to deal with problems of mineral supply was in surprisingly good repair. What had been lacking was executive will and Congressional appropriations.

Under the Mining and Minerals Policy Act of 1970, the government was under a mandate

> to foster and encourage private enterprise in (1) the development of economically sound and stable domestic mining, minerals, metal and mineral reclamation industries, (2) the orderly and economic development of domestic mineral resources, reserves and reclama-

tion of metals and minerals to help assure satisfaction of industrial, security and environmental needs. . . .

This act also commanded the secretary of the interior to submit annual reports identifying, quantifying and evaluating the impact of federal actions on the nation's nonfuel minerals resources. These reports, however, had become increasingly perfunctory and uninformative, leading the Santini subcommittee to charge in 1980: "Interior has a long record of benign neglect regarding the mining and minerals industry."

In the Defense Production Act of 1950, still on the books, the federal government had another potentially useful tool for controlling supplies of critical materials under wartime or emergency conditions, and for stimulating domestic mine production through economic incentives. Under the emergency allocation provisions of the act, the president was authorized to invoke a series of escalating steps to deal with supply interruptions of essential minerals. The first and mildest step was simply the monitoring of exports, to be followed at the president's discretion by export controls, by the imposition of domestic priorities and allocations, and as a final measure by the release of materials from the National Defense Stockpile for defense purposes or essential civilian needs.

Title III of the Defense Production Act authorizes the federal government to purchase at guaranteed prices the output of domestic mines judged essential and involving a long lead time from discovery through development to production. If market prices of the minerals rise above the guaranteed price, the producers are free to sell to higher bidders; the purpose of the act is not to assure government purchases, but to assure the developers a minimum return on investments judged to be in the public interest.

Dr. John Morgan, chief staff officer of the Bureau of Mines, found that the use of Title III provisions during the Korean War resulted in the production of $8.4 billion in critical materials, at a net cost to the government of $0.9 billion. He reports:

In a few years these programs doubled U.S. aluminum production, increased U.S. copper mine capacity by a quarter, initiated U.S. nickel mining, created the titanium industry, quadrupled U.S. tungsten mining and greatly expanded the world columbium-tantalum mining and process industries, as well as expanding supplies of many other materials for production needs and stockpiles.[1]

In 1981, Congress and the Defense Department had an opportunity to use the provisions of the Defense Production Act to develop a domestic source of cobalt, a highly strategic metal that had not been mined in the U.S. since 1971. The potential producer was the Blackbird mine in Lehmi County, Idaho, one of the rare ore bodies anywhere rich enough to sustain mining for cobalt as the primary metal rather than as a coproduct. The Blackbird mine operated under a government contract in the 1950s, but closed when the contract expired.

In 1977 Noranda Mining Inc., an affiliate of a large Canadian mining company, bought control of the Blackbird property and spent $35 million to repair and develop the mine. After four years of work, the company estimated that it could bring the mine into production at a rate of four million pounds of cobalt a year, about 20 percent of U.S. consumption of cobalt in 1980. This program would cost about $200 million and take on the order of five more years of work.

Noranda sought a contract under the Defense Production Act to sell the government cobalt at $20 a pound. The company maintained it would need this floor price and a guaranteed market in order to raise capital in a period of high interest rates and to protect itself against what it called "predatory pricing" by the world's primary cobalt producers in Zambia and Zaire.

In late 1981 the producer price for cobalt was around $17.25 a pound (down from $25 in 1979 and 1980). But in 1981 the Government Services Administration had bought 5.2 million pounds of cobalt at an average negotiated price of around $15 a pound. The government faced a dilemma.

Should it continue to rely upon the traditional producers in Africa, trusting that their governments would remain in place and that the mines would operate without interruption, or should it pay a premium for the security of a domestic supply of one of the most vital of the strategic metals? If the government decides to underwrite production at the Blackbird mine, it may face similar decisions in the case of other economically marginal cobalt mines in Missouri and California. As in so many cases, security has a price tag.

THE OUTLOOK

In its defense planning, the government must not only assure its defense contractors of ample stocks of the strategic materials that modern arms require, but in its planning it must also take into account the market impact of its major adversary, the Soviet Union. The economic planners of the Soviet Union must provide for their own mammoth defense establishment, drawing upon their own domestic production, but also using their surplus to earn hard currency in world markets.

The inscrutable Soviet traders can shift sides from buying to selling or selling to buying with no explanation, leaving it to Western market-watchers to try to discern the reasons behind the shift. In recent years the Soviets have suddenly and without explanation halted or sharply reduced sales of manganese, chromium, platinum group metals, vanadium, titanium, asbestos and lead, and have just as mysteriously become buyers of tantalum, beryllium and lithium. Were these shifts the result of new demands by the Soviet arms industry, the result of unreported mine accidents or efforts to manipulate the market? The reasons are seldom clear.

As commander in chief of the armed forces, the president of the U.S. must see to the adequate supply of critical materials for the defense industries, but he must also make sure that the defense contractors with their government money and priorities do not starve out essential civilian industries. Further, the president must, by the nature of his office, reconcile these conflicting demands not only for the term of his service, but taking into account the requirements of the next decade and the century to follow.

U.S. arms. Ronald Reagan's response to the dangerous military imbalance that he found was to push through the biggest defense appropriation in history, $200 billion for fiscal 1982, and to embark on a five-year program to upgrade and expand the major weapons systems.

The Air Force was authorized to order 100 B-1 bombers, a sophisticated aircraft consisting by weight of 41 percent aluminum alloys, 21 percent titanium alloys and 6 percent steel alloys. While the B-1 was scheduled to become the Air Force's first-line bomber in the 1980s, succeeding the aging B-52s, work will also proceed on the Advanced Technology Bomber, the so-called Stealth bomber, which is designed to succeed the B-1 as the top-of-the-line manned bomber in the 1990s.

The Defense Department explained how it had revised the long-term strategy it had inherited: "The previous Administration planned to rely on B-52s in the 1980s and to develop the Advanced Technology Bomber. . . . Building two bombers [the B-1 and the

Advanced Technology Bomber] will stimulate competition and give the Defense Department the flexibility to adjust bomber procurement in accordance with any changes in estimates of the cost and effectiveness of the aircraft."[2]

The Air Force will also add single-engine F-16 and twin-engine F-15 fighter-interceptors, with their Pratt & Whitney F-100 power plants. To build each of these engines requires an input of 5,366 pounds of titanium, 5,204 pounds of nickel, 1,656 pounds of chromium, 910 pounds of cobalt, 720 pounds of aluminum, 171 pounds of columbium and 3 pounds of tantalum.[3]

Along with these potent fighters, the Air Force will also add A-10 close-support aircraft, and AWACS aircraft, which with their elaborate radar and computer systems function as airborne detection centers and command posts. Also on the shopping list: several thousand airborne cruise missiles, and other advanced weaponry. Total cost for these Air Force weapons systems is estimated at $51.5 billion by 1986.

The Army will add M-1 tanks, M-2 and M-3 armored vehicles, surface-to-air missiles and UH-60 and AH-64 helicopters, spending an estimated $52.1 billion on major weapons by 1986.

The Navy will add to its fleet of F-18 and F-14 fighters, build Trident submarines and the missiles to arm them, attack submarines and new DDG-47 destroyers, all at a cost of $114.4 billion by 1986.[4]

Soviet arms. Even these enormous programs will be more than matched by the Soviet Union in the years ahead. The Defense Department estimates that the Soviets will continue to pour 10 percent to 12 percent of their gross national product (versus 5.6 percent in the U.S. in 1982) into weapons and defense. New tanks, armored vehicles, artillery, infantry weapons, missiles, aircraft, submarines and surface ships will roll out of Soviet factories and shipyards in a never-ending stream. In its publication *Soviet Military Power* the Defense Department observes:

> To the Soviets, defense spending is a necessity and a priority above all else. Productivity might continue to decline and the Soviets might have to face a negative growth rate, but the system of fostering massive military industrial production will continue.

The arms trade. In neither East nor West is all military production for home consumption. The international sale of weapons has developed into one of the world's largest businesses, estimated at $120 billion a year, about equaling in value the world's international trade in food. In 1980 alone, arms sales to Third World countries jumped

43 percent, to $18.3 billion, while contracts were signed for $41 billion in future deliveries.

In this commerce, the U.S. is the world leader, followed closely by the Soviet Union and more distantly by France. In all cases, the arms trade is a significant earner of foreign exchange, and for the West it is a means of recovering some of the billions of dollars transferred to oil-producing countries. Among the OPEC members, Saudi Arabia has bought heavily in the West, Libya from the Eastern Bloc, and Nigeria is considering substantial purchases. The CIA estimates that weapons sales bring in close to one-fourth of the foreign currency earned by the Soviet Union; arms are the leading currency earner for France and a significant source of strength for the U.S. dollar.

Aerospace. The space programs of the U.S. and the Soviet Union will continue to absorb vast amounts of money, manpower, scientific talent and critical materials. During the 1970s, the Soviets launched spacecraft at a rate of more than 75 a year, four or five times as many as the U.S. launched in the same period. Official U.S. sources estimate that 70 percent of the Soviet space programs serve a purely military role, 15 percent a dual civil-military function, and 15 percent is for essentially civilian purposes. The Soviets appear to be developing an antisatellite co-orbital interceptor, a spacecraft capable of intercepting and destroying other satellites. A new booster under development is expected to be able to put up very large permanently manned space stations.

The U.S. maintains its own fleet of military satellites, but the major vehicle for space operations in the 1980s will be the space shuttle, a manned reusable vehicle that rises vertically like a rocket and lands like a powerless airplane on a long airstrip. It will be used for both military and civilian purposes.

The space shuttle will be able to carry satellites aloft, hoist them out of its cargo hold and set them in independent orbit. The smaller spacecraft with their own propulsion systems can then assume new orbits or go into trajectory for travel into deeper space. The crew of the space shuttle will be able to intercept satellites in orbit and capture them or repair and refurbish them in space. On-board experiments and work labs will enable the space shuttle's crew to carry out scientific experiments in space, and to perform industrial processes, such as the growing of crystals, where the weightless environment is advantageous. Clearly, the economy and versatility of the space shuttle will open up new frontiers for work, study and the expansion of knowledge.

The implications of the space shuttle and space exploration on critical and strategic materials will be complex. The shuttle and its engines and boosters use more than 20 critical metals, from aluminum through beryllium, columbium, nickel, titanium to vanadium and zinc. The shuttles and the satellites they launch will contribute to the discovery of resources previously unknown to man. Satellite sensing, using techniques from conventional black-and-white and color photography and infrared (heat-sensing) photography to radar and lasar technology, will provide data for the construction of geological maps of a precision and sophistication previously unattainable. Thus, space-borne tools will provide geologists with new information and insights into the earth's structure and contribute to the discovery of mineral deposits.

Since satellites can follow paths without regard to the earth's political boundaries, scientists will be able to glean geological information about areas of the globe inaccessible to land-based prospectors. There is no monopoly on either science or space travel, so East and West will be increasingly knowledgeable about the other's resources.

Farther out in time is the prospect that space shuttles may lift huge payloads to be assembled as space stations. One visionary project, not too far beyond the state of the art in 1982, is the construction of a giant solar collector of a size measured in kilometers, capable of generating electricity from the sun's rays and transmitting power by microwave to earthbound consumers.

The use of strategic metals in the aerospace industry will continue to grow. U.S. aircraft builders serve not only a large U.S. market but they lead all other manufacturers in volume of export sales— $17.3 billion in 1981, a probable $18.2 billion in 1982.[5] Increasing sophistication of design increases demand for strategic metals. The Boeing 727, for instance, requires 650 pounds of titanium, while the newer and larger Boeing 747 demands 8,143 pounds. High-performance engines also use larger amounts of titanium, nickel, chromium, cobalt and columbium than older power plants. Any design reduction in the use of these supermetals tends to reduce engine performance.

Energy. The oil crisis of 1973–74 and OPEC's staggering price increases thrust the world into a new era of high-cost energy and placed a premium on the discovery of new oil reserves not under OPEC control. Much of the search has taken place offshore, from vessels that are really floating electronic platforms. One such ship may contain up to three million circuits; it tows a streamer two miles or more in length, recording signals reflected from the subsurface and flashing data to satellites for transmission to distant data-processing centers. The electronic equipment on land and sea requires a long list of precious and strategic metals: gold, silver, platinum, palladium, a great deal of cobalt and quantities of antimony, tellurides, yttrium, cadmium, samarium, beryllium, tantalum and other elements.

When the exploration teams have located the most favorable areas for drilling, new teams move into place with their tools of high-strength steels and drill bits of tungsten carbide. After the oil is found, it moves to refineries where platinum group metals serve as catalysts in the refining process to make lubricants and fuels that move through pipelines of vanadium steel to storage centers and markets.

The automobile industry in its effort to design lightweight, fuel-efficient vehicles makes increasing use of aluminum, high-strength steels and plastics, which in turn are the products of the petro-chemical industry. For greater engine efficiency and the control of emissions, the builders foresee increasing use of tiny computers to regulate carburetors and ignition systems. Computers will also be used in cars of the future to adjust suspensions for a soft or firmer ride. In fact, in an era when size will no longer mark a luxury car, the sophistication of its electronics may be the true hallmark of a luxury car.

While the construction of nuclear power plants in the U.S. has slowed markedly since the accident at Three Mile Island in 1979, other countries with fewer options are continuing to develop nuclear power as an alternative to the use of fossil fuels. In late 1981 a total of 182 atomic-powered generating plants were in operation in 21 countries and another 138 plants were under construction.[6]

These nuclear plants are big consumers of critical and strategic metals, using zirconium metal and hafnium in the fabrication of nuclear fuel rods, and superalloys to contend with the extremely high operating temperatures on nuclear generating equipment. It seems clear that the nonmilitary nuclear industry will continue to consume substantial amounts of strategic and critical metals well into the future.

REAL PROBLEMS IN THE REAL WORLD

The problems of mineral dependency cannot be easily pigeon-holed as domestic or foreign, economic or political. They are domestic *and* foreign, economic *and* political. They can be dealt with only at the highest levels of government and business. The private investor not only has a stake in the outcome, but a possible role in the solutions.

Abroad, the Soviet Union builds policy upon its growing influence in the Third World and upon its expanding military power. Says Dr. William R. Van Cleave of the University of Southern California, a leader of a Reagan transition team on national defense: "Soviet leaders now believe that the correlation of forces has shifted in the Soviet favor, and it opens a historic opportunity to extend Soviet power and influence at the expense of the West, and particularly to deny to the West the critical materials upon which its economies and hence its ultimate health depends."[7]

In the resource-rich countries of the Third World, nationalization, mismanagement and political unrest are a triple threat to the security of mineral supplies. In South Africa, internal unrest may grow in the years ahead, with unpredictable effects on that country's otherwise thriving mining sector. In Canada and Australia, democratic governments tend to place the heavy hand of domestic policy on their mineral industries. In the U.S., environmental concerns, restrictions on the use of government lands and capricious stockpiling policies inherited from the past have weakened the American mining industry.

To meet this formidable set of problems and provide reasonably secure sources of raw materials for itself and its allies in the years ahead, the U.S. can take some rational steps. Among these steps:

1. *Military renaissance.* Move promptly to rebuild the nation's military strength along the lines proposed by the Reagan Administration and substantially endorsed by the Congress.

2. *Coordination of government policies.* In the past, government policies have too frequently pulled in conflicting directions. While one set of laws on automobile emissions and industrial pollution demand increased use of chromium, the U.S. for reasons of international policy joined in an embargo on chromium from Zimbabwe (then Rhodesia) and placed diplomatic pressure on South Africa, the non-Communist world's other principal producer. The government should have an official or agency with the responsibility to weigh the

nation's conflicting objectives, point out contradictions, and bring the question of strategic-material dependency into the highest decision-making levels of government.

President Reagan's creation of a Cabinet-level Council on Natural Resources and the Environment under the secretary of the interior is a move in the right direction, but the coordination function probably should be institutionalized within the executive office of the president, with authority to cut across departmental lines.

3. *Rational use of public lands.* Controlling more than one-third of the land acreage of the U.S., much of it where nature has created both great scenic beauty and high mineral potential, the federal government should continue the moves started by Secretary of the Interior Watt to permit freer exploration for minerals. The national parks are off limits to mining and, short of the direst emergency, should remain so, but hundreds of millions of acres of other government lands could be explored without damage to the environment and their potential for mining of critical minerals weighed against other public interests. Arguments can be made against the exploitation of areas of unique historical value or natural beauty, but almost none can be made against identifying and analyzing significant mineral resources.

4. *Better management of the strategic stockpile.* While changing technology and production patterns are legitimate reasons to revise stockpile goals and procurement plans, the stockpile has been used too often in the past for short-range political purposes: to influence markets and to provide quick cash for the Treasury from the sale of "excess" materials. All too often, the surplus supplies sold off have had to be replaced later at much higher costs. While the Congress must retain ultimate control of stockpile expenditures, it need not involve itself in every administrative decision. A bill introduced by Senator Harrison Schmitt of New Mexico, the Strategic Stockpile Reform Act of 1981, deserves careful consideration. This bill would place the management of the stockpile under control of a Strategic Stockpile Commission, using the proceeds of sales of materials exclusively for the purchase of other materials, and remove the stockpile funds from the Congressional budget authorization process. This would hinder the use of the stockpile for economic or political reasons, a desirable goal.

5. *The seabed and critical metals.* The U.S. supported a United Nations resolution in 1970 declaring the resources of the deep seabed "the common heritage of mankind," a concept since effectively

seized upon by Third World nations to delay seabed development on terms acceptable to the industrial nations. If this conflict cannot be resolved in ways satisfactory to the U.S. and its allies at the United Nations Conference on Law of the Sea, the U.S. and other industrial nations have the option to form their own legal regime for seabed mining. As a last resort, that option should be exercised.

6. *Tax policies and private stockpiles*. The House Mines and Mining subcommittee observed: "An essential ingredient of a workable nonfuel minerals policy is a Federal income tax system which allows—indeed encourages—the mining industry to make the capital investments that are necessary to find, develop and produce the minerals on which our economy and national security depend." This approach can be further strengthened by tax policies encouraging the private as well as the public stockpiling of critical and strategic materials. Swedish laws according favorable tax treatments for privately held stockpiles may serve as a model for similar tax treatment for U.S. industries. Other tax-related incentives for private stockpiling might include the authorization of tax-free bonds to finance privately held stockpiles of certain essential commodities. Favorable treatment of capital gains could be extended to private investors holding critical materials as a part of a national reserve.

7. *Dealing with foreign dependency*. The U.S. can, in some cases, reduce its foreign dependency for critical materials by regulating exports of finished products and limiting nonessential uses and by offering incentives for production in cases where mines are not viable in a completely free market. But for many materials, foreign dependence cannot be eliminated. Some of the mineral-rich nations of the Third World, and particularly some in Southern Africa, share with the U.S. a common interest in two-way trade. They need technology and technical advice, food, and in some cases military aid to maintain their independence, while the U.S. has a powerful concern with maintaining access to their raw materials. These mutual interests suggest strong reasons for maintaining communication and two-way trade, but this trade can be sustained only under ground rules that demand adherence to contracts and the rule of law, including freedom from nationalization without fair compensation. These relations, however, should not be purchased at the expense of U.S. relations with Southern Africa's most important mineral producer, the Republic of South Africa. Ways must be sought to insulate the minerals trade in Southern Africa from political disruptions.

Notes

1
THE WORLD OF STRATEGIC METALS

Page
4   1. Simon Strauss, "The Role of Business in the Resource War" (speech delivered at a conference entitled "Strategic Minerals: A Resource Crisis," New York: May 22, 1981).

5   2. Subcommittee on Mines and Mining of the House Committee on Interior and Insular Affairs, *U.S. Minerals Vulnerability: National Policy Implications*, quoting the Paley Commission Report (Washington, D.C.: Government Printing Office, November 1980).

7   3. Robert J. Buckley, "Critical Materials for Industry—A Predicament That Need Not Become a Crisis" (speech delivered to the Economic Club of Detroit, January 26, 1981).

8   4. Richard C. Mulready, (statement before the Science, Technology and Space subcommittee of the Senate Commerce, Science and Transportation Committee, July 2, 1980).

9   5. Federal Emergency Management Agency, *Stockpile Report to the Congress, October 1980–March 1981*, (Washington, D.C.: October 30, 1981), p. 2.

9   6. General Alton D. Slay, "The Air Force Systems Command Statement on Defense Industrial Base Issues" (statement before the Industrial Preparedness Panel of the House Armed Services Committee, November 13, 1980), p. III–14.

10   7. Ibid, p. III–6.

12   8. Dr. William A. Owczarski, "Materials Criticality in Jet Engines" (statement before the Department of Commerce workshop on Materials Criticality in the Aerospace Industry, Gaithersburg, Md., February 9–10, 1981).

2
THE SPECIAL IMPORTANCE OF SOUTH AFRICA

Page
15   1. House subcommittee on Mines and Mining of the Committee on Interior and Insular Affairs, *U.S. Minerals Vulnerability: National Policy Implications* (Washington, D.C.: November 1980), p. 83.

17   2. Study Commission on U.S. Policy Toward Southern Africa, *South Africa: Time Running Out* (Berkeley and Los Angeles: University of California Press, 1981), p. 129.

20   3. Ibid, pp. 351–2.

21   4. Ibid, p. 357.

22   5. Senate Committee on Foreign Relations, *Impressions of Southern Africa* (Washington, D.C.: Government Printing Office, December 1979), p. 3.

22   6. Congressional Research Service, *Imports of Minerals from South Africa by the United States and the OECD Countries,* prepared for the subcommittee on African Affairs, Senate Foreign Relations Committee (Washington, D.C.: Government Printing Office, September 1980), p. xi.

23   7. House subcommittee on Mines and Mining of the Committee on Interior and Insular Affairs, *Sub-Sahara Africa: Its Role in Critical Mineral Needs of the Western World* (Washington, D.C.: Government Printing Office, July 1980), pp. 20–21.

24   8. Defense Industrial Base Panel of the House Committee on Armed Services, *The Ailing Defense Industrial Base: Unready for Crisis* (Washington, D.C.: Government Printing Office, December 31, 1980), p. 1.

25   9. Ibid, p. 25.

26   10. Chester Crocker, "Regional Strategy for Southern Africa" (speech delivered before the American Legion in Honolulu, August 29, 1981).

3
SUBCONTINENTAL CHAOS IN SOUTHERN AFRICA

Page
34   1. Robert E. Henderson and Michael A. Samuels, *Report on Zaire* (Washington, D.C.: Georgetown University Center for Strategic and International Studies, February 1978), p. 11.

35   2. John Gunther, *Inside Africa* (New York: Harper & Brothers, 1955), p. 675.

35   3. Subcommittee on Mines and Mining of the Committee on Interior and Insular Affairs, *Sub-Sahara Africa: Its Role in Critical Mineral Needs of the Western World* (Washington, D.C.: Government Printing Office, 1980), p. 4.

36   4. Alan Cowell, "At Zaire Massacre Site, the Scars and Fears Live On," *New York Times,* August 21, 1981.

37   5. *Sub-Sahara Africa,* p. 4.

39   6. Ebraham Shekarchi, *Zimbabwe,* prepared for Bureau of Mines, U.S. Department of Interior (Washington, D.C.: Government Printing Office, August 1981), p. 23.

40   7. Joseph Lelyveld, "Zimbabwe Imports Indian Craftsmen," *New York Times,* September 27, 1981.

44   8. Chester Crocker, *Report on Angola* (Washington, D.C.: Georgetown University Center for Strategic and International Studies, 1976), p. 2.

44   9. Ibid, p. 2.

4
PACIFIC PRODUCERS: MEXICO, CANADA, AUSTRALIA

Page

49   1. Least Developed Countries, or LDCs, are defined by the United Nations General Assembly as countries which in 1970 had a per capita income of $100 a year or less.

5
THIRD WORLD RALLYING CRY:
A NEW INTERNATIONAL ECONOMIC ORDER

Page

56   1. A term somewhat loosely applied to about 120 countries which are not part of the developed market economies (generally the U.S., Canada, Australia, Japan and Western Europe), or the Socialist bloc of Eastern Europe.

58   2. Rita Hauser (speech delivered before the 18th World Affairs Forum of the World Affairs Council of Pittsburgh, June 17, 1980).

60   3. United Nations Division for Economic and Social Information, *Towards a World Economy that Works* (New York: 1980), p. 52.

64   4. Investment figures compiled on request to the Bureau of Economic Analysis, U.S. Department of Commerce.

65   5. Charles Barber (speech delivered before the 18th World Affairs Forum of the World Affairs Council of Pittsburgh, June 17, 1980).

65   6. Bhaskar P. Menon, *Global Dialogue* (London and New York: Pergamon Press, 1977).

6
THE RESOURCE WAR: IT IS REAL

Page

67   1. Rear Admiral William C. Mott, *The Possibility of a Resource War in Southern Africa,* proceedings from testimony before the subcommittee on Africa, House Committee on Foreign Affairs (Washington, D.C.: Government Printing Office, 1981).

67   2. Rear Admiral William C. Mott, from his prepared statement but not included in official transcript.

69   3. James Arnold Miller, Daniel I. Fine and R. Daniel McMichael, eds., *The Resource War in 3-D—Dependency, Diplomacy, Defense* (Pittsburgh: World Affairs Council of Pittsburgh, 18th World Affairs Forum, 1980).

74   4. Michael A. Samuels, et al., *Implications of Soviet and Cuban Activities in Africa for U.S. Policy* (Washington, D.C.: Georgetown University Center for Strategic and International Studies), p. 44.

74   5. Ibid, p. 32.
75   6. Ibid, pp. 35–7.
77   7. Daniel I. Fine, "Minerals Availability—the Soviet Union and the Resource War" (paper presented to the American Mining Congress Convention, Denver, September 28, 1981).

7
SUBMARINE WEALTH: WHO OWNS
THE BOTTOM OF THE SEA?

Page
85   1. Elliot L. Richardson (speech delivered before the American Mining Congress, San Francisco, September 24, 1980).

8
THE REAGAN RENAISSANCE

Page
90   1. *Soviet Military Power* (Washington, D.C.: Government Printing Office, 1981).

96   2. Simon Strauss (speech delivered at a conference entitled "Strategic Minerals: A Resource Crisis" at the Pierre Hotel, New York, May 22, 1981).

97   3. Roy Markon (statement before the subcommittee on Seapower and Strategic and Critical Materials of the House Armed Services Committee, June 2, 1981).

99   4. James Watt (speech to the Associated Press Managing Editors, Toronto, Canada, October 23, 1981).

100   5. "It Takes a Lot of Energy to Keep Up With Interior's Jim Watt," *Denver Post*, March 1, 1981.

102   6. Congressional Record (Washington, D.C.: July 31, 1980), p. S10405.

9
THE STRATEGIC METALS

Page
104   1. Ben Bova, *The High Road* (Boston: Houghton Mifflin, 1981).

11
HOW THE MARKET WORKS

Page
141   1. *The Resource War and the U.S. Business Community*, National Strategy Center (Washington, D.C.: 1980).

13
WHAT THE FUTURE HOLDS

Page

163   1. John Morgan, "Strategic Materials Scarcities: Real and Imagined" (paper presented at the National Conference on Strategic Resources, Washington, D.C.: December 1, 1981).

166   2. Department of Defense, *The Reagan Strategic Program* (Washington, D.C.: 1981).

166   3. Dr. William Owczarsky, "Materials Criticality in Jet Engines" (paper presented at a Department of Commerce workshop, Gaithersburg, Md., February 9–10, 1981).

166   4. Cost estimates in 1981 dollars, as compiled by the *New York Times*, November 29, 1981, from Department of Defense sources.

168   5. Figures on export sales by the aerospace industry obtained on request to the Bureau of Industrial Economics, Department of Commerce.

169   6. "The Extended Nuclear Family," *Time*, October 26, 1981, p. 20.

170   7. "The Resource War and National Security" (speech delivered by Dr. William R. Van Cleave at a conference on strategic minerals sponsored by the New York Chamber of Commerce and Industry, New York, May 22, 1981).

Bibliography

1
THE WORLD OF STRATEGIC METALS

Buckley, Robert J. "Critical Materials for Industry—a Predicament that Need Not Become a Crisis." Speech delivered to the Economic Club of Detroit, January 26, 1981.

Federal Emergency Management Agency. *Stockpile Report to the Congress, October 1980–March 1981*. Washington, D.C.: October 30, 1981.

Slay, General Alton D. "The Air Force Systems Command Statement on Defense Industrial Base Issues." Statement before the Industrial Preparedness Panel of the House Armed Services Committee. Washington, D.C.: November 13, 1980.

Subcommittee on Mines and Mining of the House Committee on Interior and Insular Affairs. *U.S. Minerals Vulnerability: National Policy Implications*. Washington, D.C.: Government Printing Office, November 1980.

2
THE SPECIAL IMPORTANCE OF SOUTHERN AFRICA

Congressional Research Service. *Imports of Minerals from South Africa by the United States and the OECD Countries*. Prepared for the subcommittee on African Affairs, Senate Foreign Relations Committee, Washington, D.C.: Government Printing Office, September 1980.

Crocker, Chester. "Regional Strategy for Southern Africa." Speech delivered before the American Legion in Honolulu. August 29, 1981.

Defense Industrial Base Panel of the House Committee on Armed Services. *The Ailing Defense Industrial Base: Unready for Crisis*. Washington, D.C.: Government Printing Office, December 31, 1980.

Study Commission on U.S. Policy Toward Southern Africa. *South*

Africa: Time Running Out. Berkeley and Los Angeles: University of California Press, 1981.

Subcommittee on Mines and Mining, House Committee on Interior and Insular Affairs. *Sub-Sahara Africa: Its Role in Critical Mineral Needs of the Western World*. Washington, D.C.: Government Printing Office, July 1980.

3
SUBCONTINENTAL CHAOS IN SOUTHERN AFRICA

Cowell, Alan. "At Zaire Massacre Site, the Scars and Fears Live on." *New York Times*, August 21, 1981.

Crocker, Chester. *Report on Angola*. Washington, D.C.: Georgetown University Center for Strategic and International Studies, 1976.

Gunther, John. *Inside Africa*. New York: Harper & Brothers, 1955.

Henderson, Robert E., and Samuels, Michael A. *Report on Zaire*. Washington, D.C.: Georgetown University Center for Strategic and International Studies, February 1978.

Lelyveld, Joseph. "Zimbabwe Imports Indian Craftsmen." *New York Times*, September 27, 1981.

Shekarchi, Ebraham. *Zimbabwe*. Prepared for Bureau of Mines, U.S. Department of Interior. Washington, D.C.: Government Printing Office.

U.S. Bureau of Mines. *Minerals Yearbook*. Washington, D.C.: Government Printing Office, 1976, 1977, 1978–79 editions.

5
THIRD WORLD RALLYING CRY:
A NEW INTERNATIONAL ECONOMIC ORDER

Menon, Bhaskar P. *Global Dialogue—The New International Order*. London and New York: Pergamon Press for the Center for Economic and Social Information, United Nations, 1977.

Overseas Development Council. "Third World Development: A U.S. Perspective." New York: 1981.

United Nations Association. "Caught in the Crunch—The Changing International Economic Order and World Food Problems." New York: 1979.

6
THE RESOURCE WAR: IT IS REAL

Jordon, Amos A., and Kilmarx, Robert A. *Strategic Mineral Depen-dence: The Stockpile Dilemma*. Washington, D.C.: Georgetown University Center for Strategic and International Studies, 1979.

Mott, Rear Admiral William C. *The Possibility of a Resource War in Southern Africa*. Proceedings from testimony before the subcom-mittee on Africa, House Committee on Foreign Affairs. Washing-ton, D.C.: Government Printing Office, 1981.

Samuels, Michael A.; Crocker, Chester A.; Fontaine, Roger W.; Simes, Dmitri K.; and Henderson, Robert E. *Implications of So-viet and Cuban Activities in Africa for U.S. Policy*. Washington, D.C.: Georgetown University Center for Strategic and Interna-tional Studies, 1979.

Szuprowicz, Bohdan O. *How to Avoid Strategic Materials Short-ages*. New York: John Wiley & Sons, 1981.

7
SUBMARINE WEALTH:
WHO OWNS THE BOTTOM OF THE SEA?

Amsbaugh, J.K. "The Ocean's Contribution to the Solution of the U.S. Strategic Materials Crisis." Paper presented at the American Metals Society meeting. September 22, 1981.

Columbia University Graduate School of Business. *Columbia Jour-nal of World Business*. Winter 1980.

Cruickshank, Dr. Michael J. "Recent Studies on Marine Mineral Resources." Paper presented before the Oceanology International Conference and Exhibition. Brighton, England: March 2–5, 1982.

Dubs, Marne. "Deep Seabed Mining: Where Do We Go from Here?" *Engineering and Mining Journal*. September 1981.

Hearings on the Deep Seabed Hard Minerals Resources Act before the House Committee on International Relations. Washington, D.C.: Government Printing Office, January 23–February 8, 1978.

United Nations Association of the United States. "Issues of the '80s." 1981.

8
THE REAGAN RENAISSANCE

"It Takes a Lot of Energy to Keep up with Interior's Jim Watt."
Denver *Post*. March 1, 1981.
U.S. Department of Defense. *The Reagan Strategic Program*. 1981.
U.S. Department of Defense. *Soviet Military Power*. Washington,
D.C.: Government Printing Office, 1981.

9
THE STRATEGIC METALS

U.S. Bureau of Mines. *Mineral Facts and Problems*. 1980 edition.
U.S. Bureau of Mines. *Metals and Minerals. Minerals Yearbook*,
Volume I. 1978–79.
U.S. Bureau of Mines. *Mineral Commodities Summary*, 1980, 1981,
1982.

13
WHAT THE FUTURE HOLDS

"Arming the World." *Time*. October 26, 1981.
"The Extended Nuclear Family." *Time*. October 26, 1981.
Fine, Daniel I., and McMichael, R. Daniel, eds. *The Resource War
in 3-D: Dependence, Diplomacy, Defense*. Pittsburgh: World Af-
fairs Council of Pittsburgh, 1980.
Jordon, Amos A., and Kilmarx, Robert A. *Strategic Mineral Depen-
dence: The Stockpile Dilemma*. Washington, D.C.: Georgetown
University Center for Strategic and International Studies, 1979.
Morgan, John. "Strategic Materials Scarcities: Real and Imagined."
Paper presented at the National Conference on Strategic Re-
sources. Washington, D.C.: December 1, 1981.

Index